BOOKKEEPING
AND
ACCOUNTS
SIMPLIFIED

Moses Carson B   **ACCA (Aff) BA/EDUC, DBA**

SIXTH EDITION   **NOVEMBER 2007**

Other books by the same author;

- IGCSE Accounting
- Bookkeeping & Accounts for Beginners
- Basic Commerce
- Accounting for BGCSE
- Accounts for High School
- Accounts for O Level
- Bookkeeping & Accounts Revision
- Bookkeeping & Accounts Questions & Answers
- Simplified Accounts for Schools & Colleges
- DIY Bookkeeping

Published by: Custom Books UK Ltd
Email: custom.books@yahoo.co.uk

ISBN 978-1-906380-08-3

P R E F A C E

Bookkeeping Simplified is designed to develop the following;

- knowledge and skills of recording, classifying and summarising financial transactions.
- knowledge and skills of communication and presentation
- knowledge and understanding of some accounting terminologies, concepts, and procedures.
- positive attributes such as accuracy, neatness and orderliness
- logical thinking, as a basis for further training in Accounts.

This book is designed for the **new syllabus.** It has questions and exercises to get the learners participate in the learning processes.

It provides the explanation and necessary detail for learners to understand on their own. The language is simplified, terms and important words are highlighted, and explained.

It contains **multiple choice, short answer, and structured questions**. It also has **past paper questions** which are helpful when preparing for examinations.

CONTENTS

CHAPTER 1

INTRODUCTION

This chapter covers; **page**

1.1   Bookkeeping And Accounting

Bookkeeping is to do with the recording of business transactions.
Bookkeeping is the classifying, recording and summarising of transactions from source documents up to the trial balance. This is done by a **Bookkeeper**, who is knowledgeable about the proper recording procedure.

Accounting is the classifying, recording, summarising, analysing and interpreting business information. It stretches from source documents up to the analysis and interpretation of accounts. This is done by an **Accountant**. The work of a Bookkeeper ends at the preparation of a trial balance. The Accountant takes the process to the end by preparing the trading, profit and loss account, and the balance sheet. They also analyse and interpret, in order to tell if the business is performing well in comparison with other years or other businesses.

Some of the bookkeeping up to final accounts and the analysis is done using computers and software, which are very fast and accurate. Most of the interpretation is done by Accountants.

Accounts is a study of the system of recording, classifying, summarising, analysing, and interpreting business information.

1.2   The Accounting Cycle

The accounting cycle refers to the stages we go through when recording and processing business information. Business information is generated from activities taking place in a business. When a transaction takes place, its first recorded on source documents, then subsidiary books, to the ledger, the trial balance, adjustments are made and errors corrected, the trading profit and loss account prepared, the balance sheet written, an analysis of the information is done, and lastly an interpretation is made that guides decision making.

The Accounting Cycle is illustrated below;

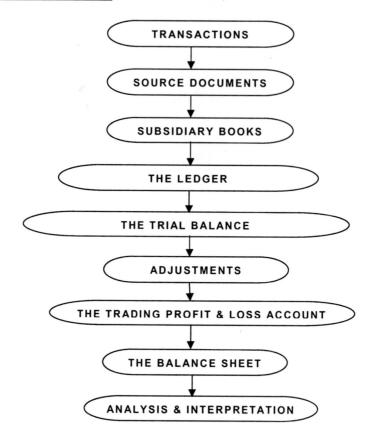

A Transaction is any dealing between the seller and buyer that involves the exchange of goods and services, or their payment. Examples of transactions are; the purchase and sale of goods, the purchase of assets, the payment for wages and salaries, rent, and other business expenses. There is always two parties to a transaction, as one is buying the other one is selling. As one is paying the other one is receiving. When a transaction takes place in a business, it's first recorded on source documents.

Source Documents
This is the source of information we record in accounts.
A document is a paper which provides written information about a transaction that took place. Documents are written as transactions take place. Documents are very important since they are the source of information we write in accounts. Documents also provide evidence in case of any disagreement between the buyer and seller.

There are several documents used from the time a buyer shows interest in goods, until the time they are paid for. For small transactions where we buy one or two units on a cash basis, the only document is a receipt or cash slip. However, for big transactions where many units are sold and bought, there are many documents used. The relevant documents in the recording of business transactions are; a receipt or cash slip, an invoice, a debit note, a credit note, a cheque, and a few others. They are explained when we come across the books where they are used.

Subsidiary Books

These are books where transactions are first recorded before being posted to the ledger. We have a separate subsidiary book for each of the different types of transactions and one that is general. They include the cashbook, the purchases journal, sales journal, purchases returns journal, sales returns journal, and the general journal. Business information or transactions are posted from subsidiary books to the ledger.

The Ledger

This is a book containing **accounts** where transactions are recorded using the double entry system. To simplify work, the ledger is subdivided into different sections which are; the debtors ledger, creditors ledger, cashbook and the general ledger. After all the transactions are recorded in the ledger and accounts balanced, we then compile a trail balance.

The Trial Balance

A trial balance is a list of balances taken from the ledger. Its aim is to prove that double entry was done properly and there is mathematical accuracy in the ledger. We then compile the **final accounts** which are the trading, profit and loss account, and the balance sheet.

The Trading, Profit and Loss Account

This is an account compiled to determine if the business made a profit or loss from its activities. It deducts the expenses from incomes. Some **adjustments** are made to the figures appearing on the trial balance. We then prepare a balance sheet.

A Balance Sheet

This is a list of assets, liabilities and capital in a business. The final stage is the analysis and interpretation.

Analysis and Interpretation

This is the use of summarised accounting information to come up with conclusions that enable us to make informed decisions. This is based on the trading, profit and loss account and the balance sheet. However, this is outside the coverage of this book.

1.3   Users Of Accounting Information

After accounting information is prepared, analysed and interpreted, it's then put to use by various groups of people as illustrated below;

USERS OF ACCOUNTING INFORMATION

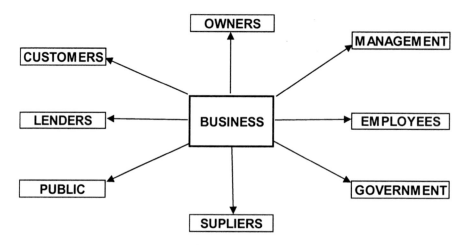

Below is a brief explanation of the different groups that look at accounting information for businesses. What is most important to them are the final accounts, plus the analysed and interpreted information.

Owners: These are the people who invest capital and own the business. In large businesses they are known as investors. They are interested in knowing how the business is performing and how well the managers have managed it. Is the business making enough profit and if not, why. How is the performance likely to be in future?

Members: If it's not a business but a club, society, or association, then they are not owners. They are members who are interested in the services provided by the organization. They are interested in knowing if the aims and objectives are being met. If they are not met then what is the problem. What can be done to improve?

Managers: These are people who run the business on a day-to-day basis. Their challenge is how to increase profits in order to keep the owners happy. If profits increase then they can ask for an improvement in their pay. So they need accounting information in order to compare and judge their performance, as well as setting future targets.

Lenders: These are people or institutions that lend money to the business and the most common are **banks**. Before they lend out money, they need to be satisfied that the business will be able to pay it back, including the interest charge. So they look at the past accounting records plus the projected future performance before lending. They also look at what the business has in form of assets, to provide as security.

Government: Their main interest is taking a proportion of profits made by businesses in form of taxes. It could take 30% of net profit, leaving 70% to the business owners. It also takes 17.5% of every sale made as VAT. The government uses tax money to provide public facilities and services like security, roads, schools, hospitals, social security, and others. However, they also use accounting information to identify the loss making but important businesses that need some assistance in terms of capital, loans, and others.

Suppliers: These sell goods and services to the business. If they sell on credit, they need to be sure the business will pay. This is indicated by the quantities sold and the profit.

Employees: These are people employed to work in a business. Their interest is to know if the business will survive and continue to provide employment, as a source of income. If accounting information shows an improvement in performance then they could ask for an increase in their salaries and wages.

Customers: These are the buyers of goods and services provided by a business. This could be a person, another business, or an institution like a school. Their interest is to know if the business will continue providing goods and services at good prices and quality. Accounting information may not be very important to an individual consumer. It's more important to a large supermarket which buys from manufacturers. If the manufacturer's business doesn't have a future, they need to identify another source in good time.

The Public: This is the general community in which the business operates. They are interested in knowing if the business is giving back anything to the community. This is because the profit made by the business comes from their expenditure. Is the business contributing to environmental protection, providing jobs, is it planning to expand or shut down?

1.4   The Importance Of Accounting Information

This refers to the circumstances in which we use accounting information. The information commonly used is in summary form and we normally refer to them as final accounts. This includes the trading profit and loss account, and balance sheet. The uses are quite many, with different objectives. Below is an explanation of some of the important ones.

1. Profit Measurement: Profit is the most important reason why the owner(s) starts a business. We get this from the profit and loss account.

2. Asses Performance: We use accounting information to tell if the business is getting better or worse, by comparing results of the current year with those of previous years. We can also judge its performance by comparing with records of other businesses.

3. Wealth Measurement: We use accounting records to identify what the business has, and to tell if it's wealthy when compared to others. This information comes from the balance sheet.

4. Taxation: The government uses accounting records to determine how much tax is paid by a business. The higher the profit, the higher the tax paid.

5. Debtor Management: We look at accounting records to know which debtors are owing, which debtors don't pay, and which debtors should not get any more credit.

6. Creditor Management: We look at accounting records to know which creditors are paid and which ones are due for payment.

7. Borrowing: The bank and other lending institutions look at accounting records to tell if the business will be able to pay back the borrowed money. They are an important guide before the bank decides to lend money.

1.5   Bookkeeping And Accounting Terms

A Business is an institution set up to carry out an activity with the aim of making profit.

Profit is the difference between the buying price and the selling price for an item. If the buying price is £50 and selling price is £70 then the profit is; £20 = 70 - 50.

The major aim of Accounting is to record business information. This information is generated from the activities which take place in a business. They include; the buying and selling of goods and services, the purchase of assets for use in the business, the selling of unwanted items like chairs and tables, the payments made for services and other business expenses, the money received, and others. These activities are referred to as **transactions**.

We have trading businesses which include shops that buy items at lower prices and re-sell them at higher prices to make profit. We also have manufacturing businesses that convert raw materials like paper into finished goods like books. They also aim at making profit since the price they charge for finished products is higher than what they spend to buy and process the raw materials.

Trade is the buying and selling of goods with the aim of making profit.

Goods are physical items used to satisfy people's wants and needs. Examples are bread, meat, clothes, cars, machines and others. In Accounting, goods bought with the aim of re-selling at a profit are referred to as **stock**.

Services are not physical items but benefits or activities done to satisfy people. Examples are entertainment, education, medical care, banking services, tourism, legal advice, and others.

A Proprietor is a person who invests their money in a business with the aim of getting profits. They own the business and if they are alone they are a **sole proprietor or sole trader**.

A Bank is a financial institution which keeps money for people, businesses, schools and government departments. It also lends money, and provides other services like exchanging currencies.

Trading Period is a length of time when the buying and selling of goods and services takes place. It could be one month or a year. At the end of this period the business finds out the total quantity of goods bought, total quantity sold, profit made, and others.

A business is always started with capital. **Capital** is the money contributed by the **owner** to the business. It's used to buy, rent or pay for the needs of the business like buildings, machinery, equipment, furniture and fittings, stock, labour, managers, and others. Capital comes from the owner's savings, or it may be borrowed from friends, relatives, or the bank.

A cash transaction is one where money is paid **before** the seller hands over goods to the buyer. Payment is made using cash, cheque, a debit or credit card.

A credit transaction is where full payment is made **after** the buyer has received the goods, or enjoyed the service. There is either non, or just part payment made before the goods cross from the seller to the buyer. A credit transaction is only made if the seller is sure they will receive their payment. When a business engages in credit transactions then it gets debtors and creditors.

A Debtor is a customer who buys goods or services without paying the whole amount immediately. When you buy on credit you become a debtor. A debtor **owes** money to the business.

A Creditor is a person or business that sells goods or services to the business on credit. Money is **owed** to a creditor.

A seller on credit is the creditor; while a buyer on credit is the debtor.

1. 6   Incomes, Expenses, And Assets

An income is money received from the sale of goods or services. The different types of income include; sales, rent received, commission earned, interest earned, and others.

An expense is money used to buy or pay for goods or services required by a business. Before a business gets income, it has to spend. For example, it has to buy stock and pay rent, before it can sell to get income. Other examples of expenses include; stationery, advertising, electricity, insurance, water, wages and salaries, bank charges, motor expenses, repairs and maintenance, and others.

According to the Law in Accounting, the affairs of the business are separated from those of the owner. Therefore, we have to separate the expenses paid by the business for the business, and those paid for the owner. Expenses paid for the owner are known as drawings and they are recorded separately.

Drawings is money or goods taken from the business for the owner's personal use.

An asset is anything owned by a business. They are used to make money or profit. We have fixed assets and current assets.

Fixed Assets: These are items bought with the aim of using them for many years. Examples are land, buildings, machinery, motor vehicles, office furniture, equipment, and others.

Current Assets: This refers to cash and the other assets easily turned into cash. This includes money on the bank account, stock and debtors. They don't stay for long in the business since their form keeps on changing as they are used to make profit. For example, when stock is sold for cash, its form changes to cash and profit is made in the process.

Multiple Choice and Short Answer Questions

1. The classifying, recording and summarising of business information up to the trial balance is ....

2. The paper that provides written information about a transaction is known as a................................

3. The items used in a business for many years are called ....

4. Money or goods taken from the business for the owner's personal use is ....

5. The money paid for goods and services used in a business is known as ....

6. Any kind of money received by a business is generally known as ....

7. Any institution set up with the aim of making profit is a.............................

8. A............................is a business from which we buy on credit, whilst a ....is a person who bought goods on credit.

9. A............................is the owner of a business.

10. A financial institution which keeps money for people is a ....

11. When goods are paid for, before exchange it's called a ....transaction

12. A.................transaction is where payment is done at a later date.

13. The buying and selling of goods with the aim of profit is ....

14. The one who buys goods sold by a business is a.................

15. Which of the following is part of the accounting cycle?

A. Ledger   B. Lenders   C. Owners   D. The public

16. Which of the following users is interested in knowing if the business can repay a loan?

A. Employees   B. Lenders   C. Owners   D. Government

CHAPTER 2.

THE LEDGER

2.1   The Ledger

The ledger is a book where **accounts** for business transactions are recorded. It has several pages and each page is divided into two, the **debit side** which is on the left hand side, and the **credit side** on the right hand side.

The word **debit** means to record on the left hand side, while the word **credit** means to record on the right hand side.

Each side of the ledger has a column for recording the **date, details, folio** and the **amount** of the transaction. A page in the ledger has columns like the ones illustrated below;

Debit side   Credit side

Date	Details	Folio	Amount	Date	Details	Folio	Amount

Please note that the columns are always already drawn in a ledger book, what may be missing are the column headings.

The **double line** at the centre of the ledger page separates the debit side from the credit side. The word debit is abbreviated with **Dr** and credit is abbreviated with **Cr**. The ledger book has many pages and each page is allocated to an account.

2.2   An Account

An Account is a statement created for recording transactions that take place between a business and a particular item, person, institution, or another business. An item can be an asset, an expense, or an income. A person can be a debtor or a creditor to the business. An institution can be a school or a government department. A separate account is created for each item, person, institution, or business.

In a real business situation each account occupies a whole page in the ledger. However, for practice purposes we write several accounts on a single page. An account has a **debit side** and a **credit side** as illustrated below;

Dr   **Cr**

Date	Details	Fo	Amount	Date	Details	Fo	Amount
			Title of Account				
	Debiting is recoding on this left hand side			Crediting is recoding on this right hand side			

Below is an explanation for each of the column headings;
- **The date column** is where we record the date when the transaction took place, not when it was recorded.

- **The details column** is where we record the name of the account where the corresponding entry is found, as explained in section 2.4.

- **The folio column** is where we record the number of the account where the corresponding entry is found. This is explained in section 2.7.

- **The amount column** is where we record the amount of money for that transaction.

Please note that the word account is often abbreviated with **A/c**.
Since the columns in the ledger book are already drawn for you, to create an account you simply draw a horizontal line where you write the title of the account. The title should be written in the middle as illustrated below;

Dr   **Cr**

Date	Details	Fo	Amount	Date	Details	Fo	Amount
			Cash Account				
7	Sales		275.00	13	Stationery		24.50

The horizontal line drawn and the double vertical line create a "T" and that's why they are commonly referred to as **"T" accounts**.

2.3   Common Ledger Accounts

We open a separate account for each item, person, or institution dealt with by the business and give it a name. The items fall in the categories of fixed assets, current assets, liabilities, capital, incomes, expenses and drawings. An account is identified by the **title** which is written at the top. Below is an explanation for common ledger accounts and what is recorded on them.

Cash are the coins and bank notes available in a business. It's used to buy or pay for business requirements like stationery, stock, and others. It's also used to provide change to customers who pay using bigger notes like one for £10.00, when buying something for £6.50.
Cash is recorded on the **Cash Account.** Cash received is debited to this account, while cash paid out is credited.

Bank refers to the amount of money remaining on a bank account, the balance. This balance is used to buy or pay for business requirements like stock, fixed assets, expenses, and others. The **Bank Account** is where we record the money deposited and withdrawn from the bank. The transactions include; deposits, withdrawals, interest earned, bank charges, and others. There are several types of bank accounts but we focus on the current account. This account is debited when the business receives a cheque, or when a deposit is made. **A deposit** is when we take cash or cheque to the bank. This account is credited when we withdraw cash or make a payment using a cheque. **A withdraw** is when we get money from the bank.

Furniture and Fittings Account is where we record the purchase and sale of items like tables, chairs, shelves, cupboards, display counters, filling cabinets, and others. The purchase of any of these items is debited, while their sale is credited to this account.

Machinery Account is where we record the purchase and sale of machines used for converting raw materials into finished products. Businesses only engaged in buying and selling may not have machines. When a machine is bought we debit and when it's sold we credit this account.

Land and Buildings Account is where we record the land and buildings belonging to the business. Whenever they are bought we debit, and when they are sold we credit this account.

Motor Vehicles Account is where we record motor vehicles belonging to the business. When they are bought we debit and when one is sold we credit this account.

Equipment Account is where we record equipment belonging to the business like typewriters, computers, photocopiers, cash registers, calculators, and others. We debit this account when one of them is bought and credit it when one is sold. However, it's possible to have an account for each of these categories of equipment. For example, if the business has several computers then it can have a separate computers account.

Purchases is the cost of stock or goods bought for re-sale, with the aim of making profit. Goods are normally bought in advance and stored or displayed until customers buy them. The **Purchases Account** is where we record stock or goods bought for re-sale. We debit this account when stock is bought.
The purchase of a fixed asset is debited to the fixed asset account.

Sales is the value of goods or services sold by the business. The **Sales Account** is where we record the value of goods or services sold. We credit this account when they sold.
The sale of a fixed asset is credited to the fixed asset account.

Stock Account is where we record goods not sold during the trading period.

Rent Paid Account is where we record the rent paid by the business. We debit this account when rent is paid.

Rent Received is income from renting out part of a building or office owned or rented by the business. The **Rent Received Account** is where we record this income. This account is credited when rent is received.

Commission Paid Account is where we record the commission paid by the business. A Commission is money paid for work done on behalf of the business. It could be paid to an estate agent for the collection of rent on behalf of the business. We debit this account when it's paid.

Commission Earned is income received in return for a service done for other people or businesses. This income is recorded on the **Commission Earned Account**. This account is credited when we receive it.

Repairs and Maintenance Account is where we record payments for repairs and maintenance of business assets. This includes; painting of buildings, maintenance of furniture and equipment, repairs to machinery or damaged stock, and others. This account is debited with the payments.

Motor Expenses Account is where we record payments for the maintenance of vehicles belonging to the business. This includes service charges, repairs, fuel, spare parts, and others. We debit this account when they are paid for.

Electricity and Gas Account is where we record the gas and electricity bills paid. The business requires electricity for lighting, cooking, heating, running photocopiers, computers and other machines. We debit this account when they are paid.

Stationery Account is where we record the stationery bought for the business. This includes plain paper, receipts books, invoices books, order forms, envelopes, pens, pencils, and others. We debit this account when they are bought.

Advertising Account is where we record the advertising expenses. This includes money spent on printing catalogues, charges for news paper, radio and television advertisement, hiring advertisers, and others. We debit this account with these payments.

Insurance Account is where we record insurance premiums. The aim is to be compensated in case of a financial loss. We debit this account when they are paid.

Wages and Salaries Account is where we record the remuneration to employees. We debit this account when they are paid.

Water Account is where we record the water bills. We debit this account when they are paid.

Bank Charges Account is where we record the fees charged by the bank. We debit this account when they are paid.

Interest Paid Account is where we record the interest paid on borrowed money, or charges for **delayed payments** when stock is bought on credit. We debit this account when it's paid, or on receipt of an invoice.

Interest Earned is income received in return for depositing and leaving money with the bank for some time. The business can also earn interest by charging debtors for **delayed payments**. This interest is recorded on the **Interest Earned Account**. We credit this account when it's received or invoiced.

Sundry Expenses Account is where we record small expenses not paid regularly, or those that are not easily classified. It is also referred to as a **General expenses** account. We debit this account when they are paid

Capital Account is where we record what the proprietor (owner) contributes to the business in either cash form or physical assets. We credit this account when this contribution is made.

A Liability is money owed by the business to other businesses, institutions, or individuals. It arises when the business buys on credit or borrows money.

Drawings Account is where we record what the proprietor (owner) takes from the business for personal use. We debit this account when they take money or physical goods.

2.4   Double Entry

The recording of business transactions in the Ledger is done in form of double entry. **Double entry** is the recording of a transaction **twice** in the ledger, once on the **debit side** and once on the **credit side** of an account. Each recording is referred to as an **entry**. The debit and credit entries are made on different accounts. For every debit entry, there is a corresponding credit entry.

The principle of double entry states; debit the receiving account and credit the giving account / the source.

This means **the receiving account is debited,** while **the account giving away is credited.** Debiting is to record on the left hand side, while crediting is to record on the right hand side of an account.

Please note that if a transaction refers to a **cheque** then it's recorded on the **Bank Account**.

2.5   The Debit – Credit Table

The Debit-Credit table shows the account to be **debited** and the account to be **credited,** for every transaction. Before we compile this table, we should know which account is the **receiver** – to be debited, and which account is the **giver/source** – to be credited. Below is an illustration using transactions for David;

1. Feb. 05   Paid rent using cash £300;

   Debit the rent paid account which is the **receiver**, and **credit the cash account** which is the **source of cash**

2. Feb. 07   Received cash £200 from the sale of goods;
          Debit the cash account which is the **receiver** and **credit the sales account** which is the **source of value**

3. Feb. 08   Bought a motor vehicle using a cheque of £20,000;
          Debit the motor vehicles account and **credit the bank account**

4. Feb. 24   Paid wages £240 using cash;
          Debit the wages account and **credit the cash account**

5. Feb. 26   Paid electricity bill of £70 by cheque;
          Debit the electricity account and **credit the bank account**

The above transactions are recorded on a debit-credit table as illustrated below;

The Debit - Credit table

	Account to Debit	**Account to Credit**
1	Rent Paid	Cash
2	Cash	Sales
3	Motor Vehicle	Bank
4	Wages	Cash
5	Electricity	Bank

Please note that all the following exercises are based on cash transactions until the end of chapter 6.

EXERCISE 2A

Using the following information, prepare a debit - credit table similar to the one illustrated above.

1st .   Bought a car using a cheque
2nd .   Paid for office stationery using cash
3rd .   Received a cheque for stock sold
4th .   Paid water bill using cash
5th .   Sold stock for cash
6th .   Paid wages using a cheque

2.6   Transactions In The Ledger

Each transaction is **recorded twice** in the ledger, once on the debit side of an account, and once on the credit side of another account. It's debited to the receiving account and credited to the giving account. Each debit entry has a **corresponding** credit entry on some other account. As we make a debit entry on a ledger account, in the details column **we write the name of the account where the corresponding credit entry is (to be) recorded**. As we make a credit entry on a ledger account, in the details column we write the name of the account where the corresponding debit entry is (to be) recorded.

From a Debit - Credit Table to The Ledger

The debit-credit table in section 2.5 is improved by adding the date and amounts for each transaction. The amount for the debit entry is the same as the amount for the credit entry as illustrated below;

	Debit		Credit	
Date	Account	Amount	Account	Amount
Feb-05	Rent Paid	300	Cash	300
Feb-07	Cash	200	Sales	200
Feb-08	Motor vehicles	20,000	Bank	20,000
Feb-24	Wages	240	Cash	240
Feb-26	Eletricity	70	Bank	70
Total		20,810		20,810

The above debit-credit table is recorded onto ledger accounts as illustrated below:

David's Ledger for February

Dr							Cr
Date	Details	Fo	Amount	Date	Details	Fo	Amount
			Rent Paid Account				
Feb-05	Cash		300				
			Cash Account				
Feb-07	Sales		200	Feb-05	Rent Paid		300
				24	Wages		240
			Sales Account				
				7	Cash		200
			Motor Vehicles Account				
8	Bank		20,000				
			Wages Account				
24	Cash		240				
			Bank Account				
				8	Motor vehicles		20,000
				26	Electricity		70
			Electricity Account				
26	Bank		70				

Please note: **1.** Each and every business has **only one account** for each item in the ledger. For example, it has only one cash account and all transactions involving the receipt and payment of cash are recorded on that single cash account. Transactions should be recorded in order of date. A transaction which took place on the 2nd of January is recorded before the one which took place on the 10th of January.

2. For practice purposes, we record as many accounts on a ledger page as it can accommodate. All we have to do is leave some few lines for each account before we record the next account below.

3. The debit-credit table was introduced just to acquaint you with the ledger. So it's withdrawn after this chapter.

EXERCISE 2B
Compile a debit-credit table including the date and amount.
Please enter the totals and they should be the same. If they are different then there is an error which should be identified and corrected.
June 1st . Bought stock for re-sale at a price of £250 using a cheque
3rd .   Purchased stationery at £22 cash
7th .   Received a cheque for stock sold at £750
12th .   Paid £350 cash for rent
15th .   Sold goods for cash £125
22nd .   Paid water bill using cash £54.

EXERCISE 2C
Using the information provided in exercise 2B and the debit-credit table prepared, record the transactions on to ledger accounts.

2.7   Folio Numbers
The word folio in Latin means page. So folio number refers to the **page number** in the ledger. Since we have many accounts on a page, our folio number refers to an **account number** in the ledger. This means that each account is given a number and it's written some where at the top of the account.

What is recorded in the folio column is the number of the account where the corresponding entry for that transaction is recorded. Therefore, **a folio number** is the number of the account where the corresponding entry is found, and it's recorded in the folio column. We abbreviate folio with **"Fo"** as you may see on some ledger illustrations in this chapter.

For example, if the business bought shop fixtures for £15,000 using a cheque, we debit the furniture and fittings account and credit the bank account as illustrated below; .

Dr							**Cr**
Date	Details	Fo	Amount	Date	Details	Fo	Amount
27	**Furniture and Fittings Account**						
7	Bank	14	1,500				
14	**Bank Account**						
				7	Furniture & fittings	27	1,500

In the folio column on the furniture and fittings account, we write the number of the bank account (**14**) since that is where we record the corresponding entry.

In the folio column on the bank account, we write the number of the furniture and fittings account (**27**) since that is where we find the corresponding entry. However, since the ledger has more than one section, a folio number may indicate the section of the ledger where the account is found.

Folio numbers help when tracing the corresponding entries in the ledger since they indicate the account and section of the ledger where it's recorded.

Folio numbers tell us **which transactions have been posted** to the ledger and which ones haven't. This is because folio numbers are only entered after double entry is completed, and that is when you know the account numbers for the two accounts involved. So the absence of a folio number means it hasn't yet been posted, or the second entry isn't yet made.

2.8   Balancing Accounts

The word **balance** refers to what **remains** after some has been removed or used. It's a process of finding the difference between the total on the debit side and the total on the credit side. The difference between the two totals is the balance on the account. In case of a cash account the debit side shows cash received, and credit side shows the cash paid out. The balance on this account is the cash remaining in the business. So our reason for balancing ledger accounts is to know the amount or value remaining in the business, for each item or account at the end of a trading period.

♦   In the case of an asset like furniture and fittings, what is bought is debited to the account and what is not required is sold and credited to the account. Our interest is to know the value of furniture remaining in the business.

♦   In the case of an expense account, we are interested in knowing the total amount **spent**.

♦   For an income we are interested in knowing the total amount **received or earned**.

♦   For a debtor, we want to know how much they still owe.

♦   For a creditor, we would like to know how much the business still owes them.

2.9   Balancing Procedure

The procedure for balancing ledger accounts depends on the number of entries on the account, and whether both sides have entries. There are slight differences which are explained below.

1.   Single Entry on One Side of Account

If an account has a single entry on only one side, that amount is the total and the balance. No addition or subtraction is required. Just draw a **double line** under it, to indicate that this figure is not to be used in any future calculations on the account. This single entry is common with the Capital account.

2.   Multiple Entries on One Side of Account

If an account has more than one entry on only one side, we simply add them up and get their total. This is the balance on the account and we draw a double line below it, as illustrated below;

Dr   **Cr**

Date	Details	Fo	Amount	Date	Details	Fo	Amount
			Furniture Account				
Jan-05	Bank		1,400				
9	Cash		250				
15	Bank		800				
			2,450				

3.   Single and Equal Amounts on Both Sides of Account

If an account has one figure on the debit side and the same figure on the credit side, then there is no difference between the two and there is no balance. We just rule off each of the two figures with a double line. For example, if we bought a small machine on the 10th of March at £450 cash and sold it off on the 28th of March for a cheque of £450. There is no profit, no loss and no balance on the account as illustrated below;

Dr   **Cr**

Date	Details	Fo	Amount	Date	Details	Fo	Amount
			Machinery Account				
10	Cash		4,500	28	Bank		4,500

4.   Different Entries But Same Totals

An account may have one entry on the debit side, two entries on the credit side, and the totals on both sides are the same. This means there is **no balance** on the account and we simply enter the totals on both sides, on the same line, with a double underline. This is common with debtors and creditor's accounts as explained in Chapter 7. Below is an illustration;

Dr   **Cr**

Date	Details	Fo	Amount	Date	Details	Fo	Amount
			Debtor- Victoria				
	Sales		750		Cash		250
					Bank		500
			750				750

Even if the numbers of entries on each side is different, we always use the same procedure provided the totals are the same.

5.   Sides with Different Totals

Real balancing is done when the two sides of the account have different totals. The aim is to find the difference between the two sides (totals). The following procedure should be followed;

i)   Add up the amounts on each side of the account to get the totals. This adding should be done twice to ensure there are no mistakes.

ii)   Record the bigger total on both sides of the account and on the same line. (leave space on the smaller side for recording the difference). A double line is drawn below each of the totals.

iii) Deduct the smaller total from the bigger total to get the difference.

iv)   Record the difference on to the smaller side as a **balance c/d** (carried down). This added difference enables both sides to have the same total.

The date for this balance should be the last date of the month or trading period.

v)   The same balance c/d is recorded on the opposite side below the total as a balance b/d. **b/d** stands for brought down, meaning it came from the previous trading period. The date should be the first date of the following trading period.

Below is an account to be balanced using the above procedure;

			Cash Account			
Capital		2,400	Wages		1,800
Sales		14,000	Furniture		5,000
			Stationery		300
			Electricity		900

a)   Adding up the two sides gives us £16,400 on the debit side and £8,000 on the credit side

b)   Record the bigger total of 16,400 on both sides and underline with a double line

c)   Get the difference between the totals; 16,400 - 8,000 = 8,400

d)   Enter the difference on the smaller side as a balance **c/d**

e)   Record the same balance of 8,400 on the opposite side as a balance b/d and that's the end of balancing.

Below is the balanced account with £8,400 as the balance.

			Cash Account			
Capital		2,400	Wages			1,800
Sales		14,000	Furniture			5,000
			Stationery			300
			Electricity			900
			Balance	c/d		8,400
		16,400				16,400
Balance	b/d	8,400				

Balancing is done at the end of each month or trading period.

EXERCISE 2D

The following transactions are for Moonlight stationers. Record them in the ledger accounts and balance the accounts at the end of March 2003.

1ˢᵗ Started the business with a cash capital of £38,000
3ʳᵈ Bought goods for re-sale at a price of £11,500 cash
5ᵗʰ Took £20,000 cash to the bank
9ᵗʰ Received cash £1,200 for sales
10ᵗʰ Paid for furniture using a cheque at £4,500
12ᵗʰ Sent a cheque to clear the telephone bill of £550
14ᵗʰ Purchased pens, paper and receipts for a total cash of £125
18ᵗʰ Sold goods for cash £5,200
24ᵗʰ Paid rent for the month using a cheque of £1,800
28ᵗʰ Purchased more goods for sale using a cheque of £8,000
30ᵗʰ Paid the water bill using cash £80

Multiple Choice and Short Answer Questions

1. The left hand side of an account is referred to as the
   A. debit side
   B. credit side
   C. reverse side
   D. none of the above
2. Transactions are normally recorded by;
   A. single entry
   B. debit entry
   C. double entry
   D. credit entry
3. The column where we record the cash for a transaction is the;
   A. date column
   B. amount column
   C. details column
   D. folio column
4. The account where we record the stock bought for re sale is;
   A. stock account
   B. sales account
   C. drawings account
   D. purchases account
5. Which one of the following is not an objective of balancing a ledger account.
   A. knowing the total spent
   B. knowing total income
   C. knowing how much to buy
   D. knowing how much a debtor owes
6.. The book where business transactions are recorded using double entry is a.............................
7. The page or account number in the ledger refers to a.....................
8. Recording on the left hand side of an account is ....
9..Recording on the right hand side of an account is......................
10.The money received by a business in return for goods sold is ....
11. Stock bought for resale is ....
12. What is meant by double entry?
13. [a] What are folio numbers?   [b] Are they of any use?
14. [a] What is meant by balancing an account?
    [b] Explain the general procedure of balancing an account.
15. Give the differences between;
[a] commission earned and commission paid   [b] rent received and rent paid

EXERCISE 2E

Record the following transactions in a debit -credit table, post them to the ledger and balance the accounts at the end of September 2001.

1st Started a business with a cash of £53,000

2nd Took £50,000 to the bank

3rd Bought furniture for £1,250

4th Purchased goods for resale using a cheque of £12,000

5th Sold goods for cash £3,200

6th Sold more goods and received a cheque of £4,500

9th Paid rent using a cheque of £350

12th Cleared the water bill using cash £54

15th Purchased stationery for cash £23

18th Received a commission of £280 cash

24th Paid cash £39 for stamps and envelops

26th Paid cash £76 for the insurance premium

28th Used a cheque of £450 to pay wages

ANSWERS

2A

Date	Debit	Credit
1	Car	Bank
2	Stationery	Cash
3	Bank	Sales
4	Water	Cash
5	Cash	Sales

2B

Date	Account	Dr Amount	Account	Cr Amount
1	Purchases	250	Bank	250
3	Stationery	22	Cash	22
7	Bank	750	Sales	750
12	Rent Paid	350	Cash	350
15	Cash	125	Sales	125
22	Water	54	Cash	54

2C

Purchases Account

Jun-01	Bank	250		

Bank Account

Jun-07	Sales	750	Jun-01	Purchases	250

Stationary Account

Jun-03	Cash	22		

Sales Account

			Jun-07	Bank	750
			Jun-15	Cash	125

Cash Account

Jun-15	Sales	125	Jun-03	Stationary	22
			12	Rent Paid	350
		.	13	Water	54

Rent Paid Account

Jun-12	Cash	350		

Water Account

Jun-22	Cash	54		

CHAPTER 3

THE CASHBOOK

This chapter covers;

3.1 Introduction

Big businesses have so many transactions and their accounts are too many to be recorded in a single ledger book. This work was too much for a single person and they were very slow. In order to speed it up, the ledger was divided up into several sections and each of them assigned to a different person. The divisions of the ledger include; the cashbook, the debtor's ledger, the creditor's ledger, and the general or nominal ledger, as illustrated below;

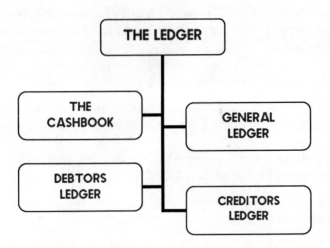

SECTIONS OF THE LEDGER

The cashbook was designed to accommodate the cash account and bank account only. So the **cashbook is a section of the ledger which contains the cash account and bank account.** Therefore, the cash and bank accounts are now recorded in the cashbook and not the ledger.

3.2   Bank Accounts

The bank keeps money for individuals, businesses, and different types of institutions. If it accepts to keep the money then it opens an account where it records the money received from the account holder, and the amount paid out.

The bank offers different types of accounts and each one has different conditions and characteristics. The most common are the current account, savings account, and the fixed deposit account. The account used by most businesses is the current account and that is what we record in the cashbook.

3.3   The Cashbook Structure

The Cashbook is similar but different from the other sections of the ledger, as illustrated below;

Dr   **Cr**

Date	Receipts	Fo	Discount Allowed	Cash column	Bank column	Date	Payments	Fo	Discount Received	Cash column	Bank column
	Debit side						Credit side				

On the **debit side** is where we record the **money received** in either cash form or bank/ cheque form. This side is referred to as the **receipts side**.   The columns we have are;

♦   The **date column** where we record the date it was received;

♦   the **receipts column** where we record the name of the account where the money came from, or where the corresponding entry is (to be) recorded;

♦   the **folio column** where we record the ledger section and account number where the corresponding entry is found;

♦   the **discount allowed column** where we record the discount allowed to debtors (chapter 10);

♦   the **cash column** where we record the money received in **notes and coins**;

♦   the **bank column** where we record the **cheques** received and cash **deposits** into the bank.

The first entry on the debit side is normally the money started with, in either cash or cheque form and it's referred to as capital.

On the **credit side** is where we record the **money paid out** by the business in either cash or cheque form. This side is referred to as the **payments side.** The columns are;

♦ the **date column** as explained above;

♦ the **payments column** where we record the name of the account where the payment went, or where the corresponding entry is found;

♦ the **folio column** as explained above,

♦ the **discount received column** where we record the discount received from **creditors**(chapter 10);

♦ the **cash column** where we record the money paid out in **notes and coins**;

♦ the **bank column** where we record the money paid out in **cheque** form.

3.4   Cashbook Contents

Below is a list of items we find on the debit side and credit side of the cashbook. However, not all of them are found in the same cashbook at the same time. Below is an illustration of what you expect to find on the debit and credit sides of the cashbook;

Dr   **Cr**

Date	Receipts	Fo	Disc. Allow.	Cash Col.	Bank Col.	Date	Payments	Fo	Disc. Rcvd.	Cash Col.	Bank Col.
	Capital						Purchases				
	Sales						Fixed assets bought				
	Debtors						Creditors				
	Fixed assets sold						Drawings				
	Other incomes				X		Deposits			X	
	Deposits						Expenses				
	Withdrawals			X			Withdrawals				X
	Overdraft c/d						Balance c/d				
	Balance b/d						Overdraft b/d				

Debit Side Contents

What we have in the receipts column are the possible sources of cash or cheques received by the business. They are accounts where the corresponding entries are found.

Capital is money invested in the business in form of cash or a cheque. It's debited to the cashbook and the credit entry is made on the capital account.

Sales is stock sold for cash. It's debited to the cashbook and the credit entry is made on the sales account.

Debtors is the amount paid by debtors for stock they bought on credit. They are explained in chapter 7.

Fixed Assets sold: When a fixed asset is sold the business receives either cash or a cheque. It's debited to the cashbook and the credit entry is on the fixed asset's account.

Other Incomes: This is income not coming from sales but other sources like rent received and commission earned. They are debited to the cashbook and the credit entries are on the income accounts.

Deposit is when cash is taken to the bank and the bank column is debited while the cash column is credited. This is a contra entry as explained in section 3.8.

Withdrawal is when cash is taken from the bank and brought into the business to meet the day-to-day cash requirements. We debit the cash account and credit the bank account. It is also a contra entry.

Overdraft is explained in section 3.11.

Credit Side Contents
What is recorded in the payments column are the items paid for, using cash or a cheque. They are, also the accounts where the corresponding entries are recorded.

Purchases is stock bought for re-sale using cash or a cheque. It's credited to the cashbook and the debit entry is on the purchases account.

Fixed Assets bought: These are fixed assets bought using cash or a cheque. They are credited to the cashbook and the debit entry is on the fixed asset's account.

Creditors is the amount paid to creditors for stock bought on credit. They are explained in chapter 7.

Drawings is money taken from the business for the owner's personal use. It's credited to the cashbook and the debit entry is on the drawings account.

Expenses is money paid for the different types of business expenses. They are credited to the cashbook and the debit entries are on the different expense accounts in the ledger.

Deposit is when cash is taken to the bank; the cash account is credited while the bank account is debited. It's a contra entry.

Withdrawal is when cash is taken from the bank; the bank account is credited while the cash account is debited. It's also a contra entry.

Below is an illustration of transactions and their entry in a cashbook;
1st   Martin started business with $340 cash and $2,500 bank
2nd   Purchased stock for resale using a cheque of $950
4th   Bought some equipment by cheque $1,300
8th   Received cash from sales $580
14th   Sold goods for a cheque of $650
17th   Deposited cash $600 on to the bank account
22nd   Purchased stationery using cash $32
26th   Drew a cheque for personal use $465

Martin's Cashbook for the month of April 2004

| Dr | | | | | | | | Cr |
Date	Receipts	Fo	Cash	Bank	Date	Payments	Fo	Cash	Bank
1	Capital		340	2,500	2	Purchases			950
8	Sales		580		4	Equipment			1,300
14	Sales			650	17	Bank	C	600	
17	Cash	C		600	22	Stationery		32	
					26	Drawings			465
					30	Balances	c/d	288	1,035
			920	3,750				920	3,750
1	Balances	b/d	288	1,035					

"C" in the folio column means contra as explained in section 3.8.

The **differences** between the cashbook and other sections of the ledger is that it has **extra columns** on both sides for **discounts,** and that the cash and bank columns are next to each other on both the debit and credit sides. An entry on the debit side increases the cash /bank balance while an entry on the credit side decreases the balances.

We should ignore the discount columns until we get to chapter 11. This leaves only the cash and bank columns on each side for recording amounts. This kind of cashbook with out the discount columns is referred to as a **two column cashbook**. A three column cashbook is one which has the extra columns on each side for discounts.

Before any entry is made in the cashbook, **we must be sure** if it's recorded in the cash or bank column, and the correct side of the cashbook.

The heading: Since the cash book is balanced at the end of each month, the heading should indicate the **month** for which it's written. The heading should have the **name** of the business and reads like; **'Martin's Cashbook for the month ended 30th April 2004'**

3.5   Balancing The Cashbook

The procedure for balancing the cashbook is the same as the one used for ledger accounts. All you have to do is ensure that you balance the cash account/ column separately from the bank account/ column.

When balancing the **cash account** in the cashbook, begin by getting the totals for the debit cash column and the credit cash column. Get the difference between the two and record it as a balance **carried down** on the smaller side, which should be the credit side. The same balance is inserted in the cash column on the debit side below the total, as a balance **brought down**. If there is no difference between the two totals then there is no balance. It means all the money was used up.

The cash account should never have a credit balance b/d. If there is a balance then it should be a debit balance. A credit balance means that payments were bigger than receipts, which is not practically possible. You cannot spend $780 when you only received $750. That is only possible with the bank account where you can get an overdraft.

When balancing the bank account, we only consider the debit and credit bank columns. We follow the same procedure used for the cash account. If it has no balance then all money deposited on the account was withdrawn or used up. A balance b/d on the debit side means that receipts were more than payments and there is an **excess** of cash on the account.

Unlike the cash account, the bank account can have a balance b/d on the credit side. This means that payments were more than receipts and the money was not enough. The difference between the two totals is what the bank lent to the business and it's called a **bank overdraft.**
However, you should be very careful when balancing the cashbook since there are normally many figures involved. To make sure there is no mistake, additions should be done **twice**; the first one should start with the figure at the top and the answer only recorded in pencil or on a rough piece of paper. The second addition should start with the figure at the bottom. If the answer is the same then it can be recorded in ink.

You can test your balancing skill by copying the entries on the cashbook illustrated on the previous page (excluding the balances and totals). You then go through the balancing process.

3.6   Source Documents

A source document is a paper which provides information about a transaction that took place. Some of the source documents for information recorded in a cashbook are; a receipt, cheque, cheque stub, and others.

When cash is received a receipt is written, and the one who paid takes the original /top copy. The duplicate copy which remains in the receipt book is what serves as the source document for cash receipts.

When cash is paid out we get the original /top copy of the receipt to prove we paid. This is what serves as a source document for cash payments. So the source document for cash received is the **receipt copy**, whereas the source document for cash paid is the **receipt received.**

A Cheque
This is a document used to withdraw money from a **bank current account**. It instructs the bank to pay a particular amount to the one written on it. On the left hand side is the cheque stub as illustrated below;

Date......................	NATIONAL BANK LIMITED		360-164
To.........................	LONDON		Date..................
Balance b/f			
Deposits	Pay...or bearer.		
Balance			
Other debits	Amount..		
Balance	....		
This cheque			
Balance c/f	POUND SHOP LTD.		
Cheque number			
0007	0007 360164 20000017664 04		

Section A	Section B

Section B above is the actual cheque we tear out of the chequebook and give to the one being paid. **Section A** is the **cheque stub**. All information recorded on the cheque is recorded on the stub as well. So effectively it's a copy of the cheque written.

Payments from a bank current account are made using a cheque. The cheque is taken by the one paid and we remain with the cheque stub. So it's the **cheque stub** that serves as the source document for cheque payments credited to the bank account.

A Deposit Slip

This is a document we use to deposit cash and cheques to the bank. It's also known as a pay–in slip. When cash or cheques are deposited to the bank, the bank stamps to confirm it received them. So the source document is the **stamped deposit slip**.

3.7   A Contra Entry

An entry is a recording of a transaction in the ledger or journal. **A contra entry** is a recording which leads to another entry in the same cashbook. **Both the debit and credit entries** for that transaction are recorded in the cashbook and this happens with deposits and withdrawals.

If it's a debit entry for a deposit in the bank column then its corresponding credit entry is in the cash column on the credit side. If it's a debit entry for a withdrawal in the cash column then the credit entry is in the bank column. We write the letter **"C"** in the folio column, which is an abbreviation for the word contra. **Contra** means that the corresponding entry is on the opposite side of the cashbook. This is illustrated on the cashbook on page 29.

3.8   Assumptions

Money received and paid out by the business is both in cash and cheque form.   Most transactions do specify how money was received or paid out. However, if the transaction states cash, it may not necessarily mean it was in cash form, it implies that it was a cash transaction and not a credit transaction. There are some transactions which do not specify how the money was received or paid out, so we have to assume or decide before recording in the cashbook.

Most **receipts** for small transactions are in cash form. Therefore, if a transaction doesn't specify then we **assume cash** and record it in the cash column.

Most **payments** by a business are made using a cheque. Therefore, if a transaction doesn't specify then we **assume a cheque** and credit the bank column.

EXERCISE 3A.

Record the following transactions in Diana's cashbook and balance it at the end of November 2003.

1st	Started business with $3,400 cash and $16,700 at the bank
1st	Bought a car for $13,500 by cheque
1st	Purchased stock for re-sale at $2,500 cash
2nd	Received a cheque for sales $1,500
4th	Drew cash $3,000 from the bank for office use.

7th   Sold goods for a cheque of $4,500
8th   Drew cash $475 for personal use
9th   Bought machinery for $14,000 by cheque
10th   Received rent $1,600 cash
14th   Deposited all cash held except $975
19th   Bought furniture by cheque $950
24th   Withdrew $500 from the bank for office use
27th   Paid electricity bill by cash $235
30th   Purchased some equipment at $7,400

3.9   Posting The Cashbook

By the principle of double entry, every transaction has a debit and a credit entry. All transactions involving the receipt/ payment using cash or cheque are first recorded in the cashbook before their second entry in the ledger. **Posting a cashbook** is the recording of the second entry in the ledger, for a transaction that was first recorded in the cashbook.

If we have an entry made on the **debit side** of the cashbook, its corresponding entry is made on the **credit side** of the account written in the details column of the cashbook. For example, sales of $580 is debited to the cash account on page 29, it's posted to the ledger by crediting the sales account as illustrated below:

Dr   **Cr**

Date	Details	Fo	Amount	Date	Details	Fo	Amount
			Capital Account				
				April 1	Cash		340
				1	Bank		2,500
			Purchases Account				
April 2	Bank		950				
			Equipment Account				
4	Bank		1,300				
			Sales Account				
				8	Cash		580
				14	Bank		650
			Stationery Account				
22	Cash		32				
			Drawings Account				
26	Bank		465				

If we have a **credit entry** in the cashbook, its corresponding **debit entry** is made on the account written in the details column. For example, purchases of $950 is credited to the bank account as illustrated on page 29. It's posted to the ledger by debiting the purchases account. All the entries in the cash book on page 29 are posted to the ledger as illustrated above.

Remember the cashbook is part of the ledger. So if both entries for a transaction are in the cashbook then they are already in the ledger and double entry is complete. **Contra entries** are not posted to any other account in the ledger.

EXERCISE 3B.

Post the cashbook you prepared in exercise 3A to the ledger, and balance each of the accounts.

3.10   Bank Overdraft

A Bank overdraft is money drawn in excess of the balance on a **current account.** Its money borrowed from the bank when you don't have enough on your current account. So the amount drawn is bigger than the balance, or amount deposited to the bank. The credit total is bigger than the debit total on the bank account. Therefore, we calculate the amount of the overdraft as the difference between the two totals. The difference is recorded on the smaller debit side as an overdraft c/d, and brought down on the opposite side as illustrated below.

For example, a business may have a balance of $450 on it's account and yet require $1,000 to buy equipment. The bank allows it to withdraw $1,000 which is more than its balance. So **the amount drawn in excess of what is on the account is an overdraft**, and in this case it's
$550 (1,000 - 450) as illustrated below;

Dr								Cr
Date	Receipts	fo	Cash	Bank	Date	Payments	fo	Cash	Bank
	Sales			450		Equipment			1,000
	Overdraft	c/d		550					
				1,000					1,000
						Overdraft	b/d		550

Please **note** that this overdraft is only possible with the bank column/ account, and not cash account.

Multiple Choice and Short Answer Questions

1.   All these are source documents for the cashbook except
A. a receipt   B. cheque stub
C. an invoice   D. a cheque
2. An overdraft is when the bank account has a ....balance.
A. Credit   B. Debit   C. Zero   D. Big
3.   A contra entry is made for a
A expense   B. invoice   C. cash deposit   D. purchases
4.   If a transaction doesn't specify how payment was made we assume
A.   cash   B. cheque
C. cash column   D. none of the above
5. Posting from the cashbook means making......................in the ledger.
A. Double entry   B. Contra entry
C. Two entries   D. One entry
6.   Which of these is a source for debits to the bank account?
A. Deposit slips   B. Withdrawal Slips
C. Cheque stubs   D. Bank statements
7. Which of the following is not recorded on the credit side of the cashbook?
A. Fixed Assets Bought   B. Fixed Assets Sold
C. Drawings   D. Purchases
8. Most payments by big companies are recorded in the .... column
A. Cash   B. Bank   C. Discount   D. Folio
9. A....................entry is where the debit and credit entries of a transaction
are recorded in the cash book.
10. When money is taken from the cash box and deposited with the bank, we
debit.........................account and credit........................account.
11. [a] What is a cashbook?
     b]   Why is it referred to as a two column cashbook?
12. What are the differences between the following?
[a] a deposit and a withdrawal of cash
[b] cash account and bank account
[c] bank balance and bank overdraft
[d] a receipt and a cheque.

EXERCISE 3C.

You are required to record the following transactions in Sinclair's
cashbook and post to the ledger for the month of March 2005.
1st Started business with cash $14,350
2nd   Purchased stock at $9,500 cash
4th   Sold goods for a cheque of $7,500
7th   Paid for equipment using a cheque of $4,150
9th   Drew all cash from the bank for office use
10th Bought an old car at $6,000
13th Received a cheque for goods sold at $840
15th Took $250 cash for personal use
18th Received rent $2,200 by cheque
20th Purchased more stock for re-sale by cheque $2,150

23rd Sold goods for cash $460
25th Received a cheque for stock sold $1,735
26th Cleared electricity bill using a cheque of $193
29th Purchased stationery by cheque $125

EXERCISE

3D. In January 2004, the following transactions were undertaken by Grace's Beauty Salon.   Record them in a cashbook, balance it, and post from the cashbook to ledger accounts.

1st   Sold goods for cash to Arthur for $2,560.
1st   Paid wages cash $150.
2nd   Bought goods from David paying cash $350.
4th   Received a cheque of $310 for goods sold.
6th   Drew a cheque of $120 to pay wages.
7th   Sold goods for $500 to Christine receiving payment by cheque.

10th   Paid for small equipment by cheque $200
13th   Took cash for personal use, $365.
15th   Purchased goods for cash $400.
16th   Paid rent by cash $250.
17th   Paid cash to bank $750.
21st   Sold the equipment for $200 cash.

EXERCISE 3E.

Enter the transactions below in Samson's cashbook for the month of May and post to the ledger. On 1st May Samson had a capital of $560 in cash form and $8,400 at the bank.

1st   Samson drew cash for his personal use $240
2nd   Received cash from sales $400
3rd   Paid postage by cash $20
5th   Cash purchases for $200
6th   Sold goods and received a cheque of $1,175
12th   Received cash for goods sold at $580
14th   Paid cash $180 for the electricity bill.
14th   Settled the rent bill by a cheque of $420
17th   Received interest by a cheque of $250
18th   Bought stock using a cheque of $370
20th   Paid $100 cash for stationery
25th   Received a commission of $500 by cheque.
28th   Bought a personal car at $650 using a cheque
30th   Took $700 cash to the bank

ANSWERS

3A Diana's Cashbook for November 2004

Date	Receits	Cash	Bank	Date	Payments	Cash	Bank
1	Capital	3,400	16,700	1	Motor Car		13,500
2	Sales		1,500	1	Purchases	2,500	
4	Bank	3,000		4	Cash		3,000
7	Sales		4,500	8	Drawings	475	
10	Rent Received	1,600		9	Machinery		14,000
14	Cash		4,050	14	Bank	4,050	
24	Bank	500		19	Furniture		950
	Overdraft c/d		12,600	24	Cash		500
				27	Electricity	235	
				30	Equipment		7,400
					Balance c/d	1,240	
		8,500	39,350			8,500	39,350
	Balance b/d	1,240			Overdraft b/d		12,600

3B The Ledger

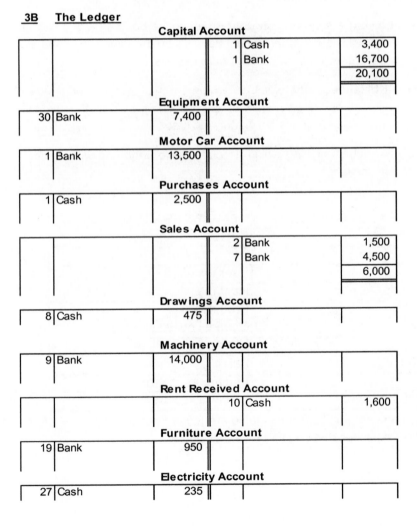

Capital Account

				1	Cash	3,400
				1	Bank	16,700
						20,100

Equipment Account

30	Bank	7,400			

Motor Car Account

1	Bank	13,500			

Purchases Account

1	Cash	2,500			

Sales Account

				2	Bank	1,500
				7	Bank	4,500
						6,000

Drawings Account

8	Cash	475			

Machinery Account

9	Bank	14,000			

Rent Received Account

				10	Cash	1,600

Furniture Account

19	Bank	950			

Electricity Account

27	Cash	235			

CHAPTER 4.

THE TRIAL BALANCE

4.1   Introduction

A Trial Balance is a list of all balances extracted from the ledger, including the cashbook. A trial balance is compiled or prepared after all accounts have been balanced and this is normally at the end of the trading period.

The balances on the trial balance are arranged according to whether they are debit or credit balances.

A debit balance is the one **brought down** on the **debit side** of an account. It may be the only figure on the account and it's on the debit side. If the account has several entries on only the debit side, then it's their total.

A credit balance is one which is **brought down** on the **credit side** of an account. It may be the only figure on the account and it's on the credit side. If the account has several entries on only the credit side, then it's their total.

Below is a table showing which accounts have debit and which ones have credit balances;

DEBIT BALANCE ACCOUNTS	CREDIT BALANCE ACCOUNTS
Fixed assets	Capital
Cash	
Bank	Bank overdraft
Expenses	Incomes
Debtors	Creditors
Stock	Current liabilities
Drawings	Long-term liabilities
Purchases	Sales
Sales returns	Purchases returns
Discount allowed	Discount received

Any items not familiar on this table are found in chapters 5 to 10. Accounts without balances don't appear on a trial balance.

4.2   Trial Balance Structure

A trial balance can be compiled horizontally in the ledger but we shall stick to the vertical format which requires 3 columns. In the first column we write the name of the account where the balance came from. In the second column we record debit balances, and the last column we record credit balances. The two columns are then totaled as illustrated below;

Trail Balance for Moon Light Stationers as at the 31st March 2003		
Account Names	Debit Balances	Credit Balances
Cash	6,050	
Bank	12,695	
Capital		38,000
Purchases	19,500	
Sationery	125	
Sales		6,400
Rent received		1,200
Rent paid	1,800	
Furniture and Fittings	4,500	
Water	80	
Telephone	850	
Totals	45,600	45,600

You have to ensure that **all balances** appear on the trial balance. You could start with those in the cashbook and then record those in the ledger. The balance for the first account in the ledger should be written first and follow their order until you get to the last one.

The Heading of a trial balance should contain **the name of the business**, the words **"as at "**, and lastly **the date** on which it's prepared. The date is normally the last day of the trading period. This is illustrated on the trial balance above.

The most important reason for preparing a trial balance is to check if the process of double entry in the ledger was done properly. It also checks to ensure that additions and subtractions done during the balancing of accounts were done properly. This is proved if the debit total is equal to the credit total. That is when the trial balance is said to have **balanced**. If the trial balance totals on the two sides are different then it has not balanced. This means there is an **error(s)** which must be investigated and corrected before the trial balance can balance.

Please note that the trial balance is made up of closing balances, with the exception of stock which is the opening balance. This is the stock balance at the beginning of the period. If a current asset like bank has an **overdraft** then it's classified among the current liabilities. So the arrangement of balances on the trial balance is based entirely on whether it's a debit or credit balance.

EXERCISE 4A

The following balances are taken from the books of Primrose Traders for the month ended May 2006. You are required to prepare a trial balance

Cash	4,840	Capital	33,100	Purchases	9,500
Bank	12,570	Machinery	14,500	Sales	17,250
Furniture and fittings		8,400	Sundry expenses	540.	

EXERCISE 4B

You are required to compile a trial balance using the following balances for the month of June 2004;

Cash	1,245	Capital	29,000	Purchases	9,850
Wages	2,350	Sales	14,355	Water	245
Machinery	24,700	Stationery	170	Telephone	490
Furniture and fittings		7,230	Bank overdraft	2,925	

4.3   Investigating The Causes Of Difference

The presence of a difference among the totals means the trial balance has exposed one or more errors. The errors could be on the trial balance itself, in the ledger (including the cashbook), or in subsidiary books (chapter 7).

Below is a procedure to follow when investigating the causes of difference. It's arranged in order of steps 1 to 6. If step 1 doesn't solve the problem then we continue to step 2, step 3, and so on until we solve the problem, and the two totals are the same.

i). We **start by re-adding** the debit and credit balances to confirm the totals are not the same.

ii). We then **check if the actual debit and credit balances** in the ledger are the ones on the trial balance, and are in the **right place.** We check one balance at a time starting with the cashbook and continue till the end of the ledger. For every balance in the cashbook or ledger, we must **compare** it to its match on the trial balance and ensure there is no difference in the figures. To avoid skipping any balances, we should follow the order of arrangement of accounts in the ledger. Any errors discovered are corrected and re-adding the affected sides could solve the problem.

iii). **Find the difference between the two totals**. If the difference is equal to any single amount among the transactions then it's very likely that transaction was entered only once in the ledger. Check for the double entry of that transaction and if one of the entries is missing then record it on the right account. We should then have a new balance on the affected account. Enter the corrected balance for this account and the affected side of the trial balance re-added. This may solve the problem.

iv). **If the difference is twice** any particular amount among the transactions then the error is likely to be **debiting or crediting a transaction twice** in the ledger. For example, debiting the rent paid account and debiting the cash account with the same amount when cash was paid for rent.

This is corrected by shifting the debit entry on the cash account to the credit side. This is done by **not crossing out** the debit entry but by **doubling the amount** and recording it on the credit side before the correct balance is got. Enter the corrected balance for this account and the affected side of the trial balance re-added. This may solve the problem.

v). **Check the balancing** on individual accounts in the ledger. Confirm if the addition and subtraction was done properly. Affected balances in the ledger should be corrected on the trial balance. Re-adding the affected sides could solve the problem.

vi). Finally, **all transactions should be checked** starting in subsidiary books (chapter 7). You have to ensure that both entries were made using the correct amount, on the correct account, and the correct side. Affected accounts should be re-balanced, and the corrected balances replace the wrong ones on the trial balance. The affected side(s) of the trial balance should be re-added.

The last procedure should leave any remaining problems solved and the trial balance having equal totals.

Multiple Choice and Short Answer Questions
1. A trial balance is a
A. ledger account   B. list of balances
C. final account   D. none of these

2. Which of the following doesn't appear on the debit side of the trial balance?

A. incomes   B. assets   C. expenses   D. drawings

3. All the following have credit balances except

A. capital   B. liabilities   C. incomes   D. assets

4. One of the uses of a trial balance is to

A. identify transactions omitted   B. expose arithmetical errors

C. show the financial position   D. show the gross profit.

5. Which of the following has a debit balance?

A. Capital   B. Liabilities   C. Expenses   D. Incomes.

6. Which of the following is recorded on the credit side of the trial balance?

A. Incomes   B. Expenses   C. Assets   D. Drawings.

7. The totals of a trial balance

A. should never agree   B. should always be the same

C. may agree   D. should be different

8. Give the differences between a debit balance and a credit balance.

9. Which steps do you go through when preparing a trial balance?

10. Explain the procedure you go through if the trial balance does not balance.

EXERCISE 4C

Write a cashbook, post to the ledger, balance the accounts, and extract a trial balance for Mark Traders for the month of August 2004, from the following transactions;

1ˢᵗ *Started business with cash $375 and bank $25,500*

4ᵗʰ *Bought goods for resale by cheque $18,500*

5ᵗʰ *Sold goods for $440 cash*

6ᵗʰ *Purchased shop fittings by cheque $5,200*

8ᵗʰ *Bought stationery at $85 cash*

9ᵗʰ *Paid for business license at $140 cash*

10ᵗʰ *Received a cash commission of $150*

11ᵗʰ *Sold goods for a cheque of $12,000*

12ᵗʰ *Purchased equipment by cheque $7,640*

14ᵗʰ *Paid advertising expense by cash $83*

15ᵗʰ *Bought more stock by cheque $4,300*

18ᵗʰ *Sold goods for a cheque of $6,000*

20ᵗʰ *Paid rent by cheque $1,200*

22ⁿᵈ *Purchased stationery for $20 by cash*

23ʳᵈ *Paid wages by cheque $540*

25ᵗʰ *Drew cash for personal use $150*

26ᵗʰ *Paid $87 for general expenses by cash*

28ᵗʰ *Received a small cheque for interest of $95*

30ᵗʰ *Deposited $400 cash into bank.*

EXERCISE   4D

Record the following transactions in Valencia's cashbook and ledger, balance the accounts and extract a trial balance for the month of January 2001.

1st   Started business with $5,000 cash and $95,000 at the bank
2nd   Bought a new car at $45,000 by cheque
3rd   Purchased goods for resale at $24, 000 by cheque
4th   Sold goods for $7,800 cash
7th   Paid motor car insurance at $350 cash
8th   Received $10,000 cash for goods sold
10th   Cleared the water bill of $135 by cash
11th   Deposited $15,000 on to the account
12th   Bought furniture by cheque $6,700
14th   Purchased equipment at $5,500
18th   Received a commission of $165 by cheque
19th   Bought more stock at $18,500 by cheque
20th   Cleared the electricity bill of $345 by cash
23rd   Paid $200 for stationery by cheque
25th   Received cash $7,000 for sales
28th   Purchased a new Motor Bike at $12,500 by cheque.
29th   Paid rent by cash $2,100
29th   Bought a new machine at $8,000 cash
30th   Received a cheque of $9,500 for goods sold
31st   Purchased new furniture by cheque $10,000.

ANSWERS

4A

Primrose's Trial Balance as at 31st May 2006

	Debit		Credit
Cash	4,840	Capital	33,100
Bank	12,570	Sales	17,250
Purchases	9,500		
Furniture & Fittings	8,400		
Machinery	14,500		
Sundry expenses	540		
	50,350		50,350

4B

Trial Balance as at 30th June 2004

Particulars	Debit	Credit
Cash	1,245	
Purchases	9,850	
Machinery	24,700	
Furniture&Fittings	7,230	
Telephone	490	
Wages	2,350	
Stationery	170	
Water	245	
Capital		29,000
Sales		14,355
Bank overdraft		2,925
	46,280	46,280

CHAPTER 5

THE TRADING, PROFIT AND LOSS ACCOUNT

5.1   Introduction

After the trial balance has confirmed double entry and mathematical accuracy in the ledger. We then compile a trading account, and a profit and loss account to find out if the business made a profit or a loss. **The success** of a business is measured by the amount of profit made.

Profit is the excess income remaining after deducting business expenses, or the surplus of income over business expenses. If the business received more income than its expenses then it's said to have made **a profit**. If it has more expenses than income then it's said to have made **a loss**. Profit is classified as gross profit and net profit.

Gross Profit is the difference between the buying price (cost) and the selling price of stock sold. This excludes the other business incomes and expenses. The buying price of stock sold is the same as the cost of sales.

Cost price is the price at which stock is bought.

Selling price is the price at which stock is sold. Selling price is got by adding a **mark-up** to the cost. **Mark-up** is the amount or percentage added to the cost in order to get the selling price. The mark-up is often worked out as a percentage of the cost price.

For example, if the cost price is $500 and the mark up is 20%
500 x 20% = 100.   Therefore the selling price is 500 + 100 = $600.
    The short cut is; Since 500 is 100%, you add 20% to 100% to get 120%.

You then multiply as follows;

       $500 x 120% = $600.
If the selling price is **higher** than cost price then the business makes a Gross Profit. If the cost price is **higher** than selling price then the business makes a **Gross Loss**.

Net Profit is got by deducting all the **expenses** from the **incomes** of the business. It's the excess of total income over business expenses. The incomes of the business include gross profit, commission earned, interest earned and discount received. The expenses are many and they include rent paid, wages and salaries, stationery, insurance, and others.

Net Profit is the reward to the owner for the risk and effort of starting and running a business. It's said to be a risk because they could make a loss and the owners loose their investment. Please note that if the expenses exceed the incomes then it's a **net loss**.

Gross profit is worked out on a trading account, while net profit is calculated on a profit and loss account.

5.2   The Trading Account

A Trading Account is a final account prepared to establish the amount of gross profit or gross loss made by a business. It's an arrangement of figures where the cost of sales is deducted from the sales income. However, before we get the cost of sales, we have to add opening stock to purchases to get the value of goods available for sale, and then deduct closing stock. A trading account can be compiled using the horizontal format but we shall stick to the vertical format as illustrated below;

Jackson's Trading Account for the month ended 30th August 2003		
Sales		74,250
Opening stock	1,020	
Purchases	+ 61,000	
Goods available for sale	62,020	
Closing stock	- 14,000	
Cost of sales		- 48,020
Gross Profit		**26,230**

Please note that sales, opening stock and purchases come from the trial balance. Closing stock is derived from stock taking as explained in **5.3**.

Goods available for sale; is the value of stock available for sale during the period and it's got by the formula;

Goods available for sale = opening stock + purchases.

Cost of sales is the cost price of **stock sold** and it's got by the formula;

Cost of sales = goods available for sale - closing stock

The complete formula is;

Cost of sales = opening stock + purchases - closing stock

Gross Profit is derived by deducting the cost of sales from sales. It's a gross profit if the answer is **positive**. If the answer is **negative** then it's a **gross loss**. This means that selling price was lower than cost price. This should be avoided in business since we aim at profit.

However, if the business doesn't have opening stock and no closing stock, the purchases cost becomes the cost of sales. So we deduct purchases from sales to get gross profit as illustrated below;

Sales	3,290
Purchases	-1,630
Gross Profit	1,660

The general formula is; **Gross Profit = Sales - Cost of Sales.**

5.3   The Stock Account

This is an account where we record the value of stock not sold by the end of a trading period.

The cost of stock bought for re-sale is recorded on the **purchases account,** while the proceeds from stock sales are recorded on the **sales account**.

Opening Stock is the value of goods available at the start of a trading period. If a business has been operational then it's brought forward from the previous trading period.

Closing Stock is the value of stock not sold by the end of a trading period and it's got by stock taking.

Stock taking is the process of **counting stock** and valuing it at its **cost price**. For example, if stock not sold is; 105 packets of sugar each costing $1.50, 83 packets of salt each costing $0.80, and 62 bottles of Coke each costing $3.00. The closing stock figure is;
(105 x 1.50) + (83 X 0.80) + (62 x 3.00)
        = 157.5 + 65.4 + 186 = **$408.9.**

The closing stock for one year is the opening stock for the following year. So the difference is; opening stock is at the beginning, while closing stock is at the end of the period. **Please remember** that the stock figure on the trial balance is always the opening stock.

Opening stock is transferred to the trading account by crediting the stock account as illustrated below, and recording it in the debit column of the trading account as illustrated on the previous pages.

Stock Account						
Bal (opening stock)	b/d	1,020	To Trading a/c			1,020
Stock taking		**14,000**	Bal (closing stock)	c/d		14,000
		15,020				15,020
Balance	b/d	14,000				

Closing stock is introduced in the books using a journal entry as explained in chapter 9. It's **debited** to the stock account and when we balance it, **the stock taking figure is the closing balance** as illustrated above. The credit entry should be on the horizontal trading account. However, since we are using the vertical trading account, we record it in the debit column as a negative figure. So it's deducted from the goods available for sale before we get the cost of sales.

The heading of a trading account specifies whose it is, the words "for the month or year ended", and the actual month or year. An example is; "Jackson's Trading Account for the month ended 30th August 2003", as indicated on the trading account on page 46.

EXERCISE 5A.
From the following balances, prepare a trading account for Regina for the month ended February 2005; sales $14,650, opening stock $1,440, purchases $11,130 and closing stock is $1,780.

5.4   The Profit And Loss Account

The Profit and Loss Account is compiled to find if the business made a net profit or net loss. This is determined by deducting business expenses from its incomes. This account can be compiled using the horizontal method but we shall stick to the **vertical format** as illustrated below;

Jackson's Profit & Loss Account for the month ended 30 August 2003		
Gross Profit		26,230
Commission Earned		155
Interest Received		150
Total Income		26,535
Operating Expenses		
Wages	3,380	
Rent Paid	2,400	
Stationery	200	
Telephone	270	
Carriage outwards	220	
Water	120	
Sundry expenses	317	
Total Expenses		6,907
Net Profit		**19,628**

To prepare a profit and loss account, you start with gross profit which is derived from the trading account. You add other incomes to get total income. You then list all the operating expenses and find their total. Total expenses is recorded directly below total income. You deduct total expenses from total incomes and the answer is either a net profit or loss. It's a net profit if the answer is positive and a net loss if it's negative.

Carriage outwards is the cost of transporting stock sold to a buyer and this is normally done if they bought in a large quantity. If the buyer doesn't pay for this then it's incurred by the business and included on the **profit and loss account as an expense**.

Carriage inwards is the cost of transporting purchased stock into the business' premises. It's added to the purchase price in order to get the total cost of purchases. It's recorded on the **trading account.**

Drawings is a **personal** and not a business expense. So it doesn't appear on the profit and loss account.

The heading of a profit and loss account should specify the owner, the words; **"for the month or year ended"**; and the actual month or year, as illustrated above.

EXERCISE 5B.

Prepare a profit and loss account for Preston for the month ended April 2005 from the following figures; Gross Profit $2,390, wages $580, stationery $120, advertising $75 and general expenses $105.

5.5   The Trading , Profit And Loss Account

This is a combination of the trading account with the profit and loss account. This is how it's normally presented. You shouldn't expect to find them separated.

The two are combined using **gross profit or loss** that is found on both.
It's the **end figure** on the trading account, and the **starting figure** on the profit and loss account as illustrated below;

Jackson's Trading, Profit & Loss Account for the month ended 30 August 2003		
Sales		74,250
Opening stock	1,020	
Purchases	+ 61,000	
Goods available for sale	62,020	
Closing stock	- 14,000	
Cost of sales		- 48,020
Gross Profit		26,230
Commission Earned		155
Interest Received		150
Total Income		26,535
Operating Expenses		
Wages	3,380	
Rent Paid	2,400	
Stationery	200	
Telephone	270	
Carriage outwards	220	
Water	120	
Sundry expenses	317	
Total Expenses		6,907
Net Profit		**19,628**

When we combine the two, the heading is also adjusted.

Therefore, a Trading, Profit and Loss Account is a final account prepared to determine the gross and net profit or loss made by a business. This account is also known as an **income statement**. A statement that shows the income of the business.

5.6   The Importance of A Trading, Profit And Loss Account

1. The most important aim is to find if the business made a profit or loss. This information is of much interest to all users of accounts.

2. It shows the **impact** of trading activities on the **financial position** of a business. If there is a net profit then the capital will increase and if there is a net loss then it decreases.

*EX5C. From the trial balance presented below, **prepare** a trading account and a profit and loss account.*
The Trial Balance of Major and Company at 31st May 2006

DETAILS	DR	CR
Capital		4,300
Creditors		1,711
Debtors	2,631	
Land and Buildings	1,500	
Equipment	1,582	
Stock	908	
Sales		9,791
Cash at bank	56	
Cost of goods sold-purchases	56	
Discount Allowed	56	
Discount Received		79
Rates and Insurance	260	
Wages and Salaries	2,571	
Advertising	243	
	15,881	15,881

Multiple Choice and Short Answer Questions

1. Gross profit is equal to
A. Sales less purchases   B. Cost of goods sold less expenses
C. Sales less total expenses D. Sales less cost of goods sold
2. Net profit is equal to
A. Sales less cost of goods sold B. Cost of goods sold less expenses
C. Total income less expenses.   D. Opening stock less closing stock
3. Gross profit is calculated on the
A Balance sheet   B. Trading account
C. Trial balance   D. Profit and Loss account.
4. Net profit is calculated on a
A. Balance sheet   B. Trading account
C. Profit and Loss Account   D. Trial balance.
5. Calculate gross profit from the following figures: Sales 1, 950; closing stock 200; purchases 850;   opening stock 420.

A. $480   B. $880   C. $520   D. $700

6. Cost of sales is equal to
A. Sales minus cost of sales
B. Purchases plus opening stock minus sales
C. Gross profit minus income
D. Opening stock plus purchases minus closing stock

7. Which one of the following does not appear on the trading account?
A. Wages   B. Purchases   C. Sales   D. Stock

8. Closing stock is found by
A. Depreciation   B. a fixed percentage of sales
C. Stock taking   D. Deducting purchases from sales

9. Which of the following appears on the trading account?
A. Carriage inwards   B. Carriage outwards
C. Motor expenses   D. Drawings

10. Which one appears on both the trading account and profit and loss account?
A. Net profit   B. Operating expenses
C. Gross profit   D. Closing stock.

11. The stock item on the trial balance refers to?
A. Opening stock   B. Purchases
C. Sales   D. Closing stock.

12. Net profit plus expenses equals?
A. Opening stock   B. Cost of sales
C. Total income   D. Closing stock.

13. Goods available for sale is equal to opening stock plus?
A. Purchases   B. Cost of sales
C. Sales   D. Closing stock

14. The difference between the   cost price and selling price is?
A. Retail price   B. mark-up
C. loss   D. net profit

EXERCISE 5D.

The following balances are for Nancy for December 2005. You are *required* to compile her trial balance, calculate her capital, prepare a trading, profit and loss account.

Cash	$1,272	Bank	$43,700
Furniture and fittings	$13200	Equipment	$9,890
Opening stock	$16,510	Purchases	$78,740
Closing stock	$8,750	Rent Paid	$6,300
Commission earned	$2,735	Advertising	$950
Water	$795	Wages	$2,850
Electricity	$1,644	Sales	$143,550

EXERCISE 5E.

Clifford started a business on the 1st of June 2002 with $1,350 cash and $15,000 at the bank.
2nd Bought stock for re-sale using a cheque of $7,400

3rd Paid for furniture for $3,500 by cheque
4th Cleared the telephone bill of $185 by cash
5th Sold goods for $4,350 by cheque
7th Paid advertising expenses by cash $110
8th Paid cash $425 for repairs
10th Purchased stationery for $250 cash
13th Paid the electricity bill of $285 cash
14th Used cash $80 to pay for water
15th Took $1,500 to the bank
16th Purchased more stock for $6,500 by cheque
18th Received a commission of $300 in cash
19th Received a cheque of $3,200 for sales
20th Paid rent of $1,300 by cash
24th Received a cheque of $750 for rent from tenant
27th Sold stock for cash $5,800
28th Paid wages $550 cash
29th Received a cheque of $3,350 for goods sold
His closing stock was $290
You are required to write up
-a cash book,
-post to the ledger,
-extract a trial balance,
-and the trading, profit and loss account at the end of June

ANSWERS

5A

Regina's Trading Account for
the month ended 28th Feb 2005

Sales		14,650
Opening Stock	1,440	
Purchases	11,130	
	12,570	
Closing Stock	1,780	
Cost of sales		10,790
Gross Profit		**3,860**

5B

Preston's Profit & Loss Account for
the month ended 30th April 2005

Gross Profit		2,390
Expenses		
Wages	580	
Stationery	120	
Advertising	75	
General Expenses	105	
		880
Net Profit		**1,510**

THE BALANCE SHEET

This chapter covers:

6.1   Introduction

A balance sheet is a statement showing the financial position of a business at a particular date. The financial position is seen by **comparing** what the business owns in form of assets, against what it owes in form of liabilities and capital. So it's also defined as a list of assets, liabilities and capital in a business.

The assets are classified as fixed and current.
Fixed Assets are items bought for use in a business for several years. Some of them last forever, whereas others are sold off as second hand or thrown away when they have no more use. They include land and buildings, motor vehicles, machinery, equipment, furniture and fittings, and others.

Current Assets refers to cash and the other assets easily turned into cash. They are held with the aim of making profit as they are converted from one form into another.

<u>The changing form of Current Assets</u> is illustrated below;

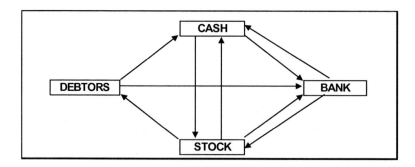

Cash becomes bank when it's deposited and bank becomes cash when it's withdrawn. Cash or bank becomes stock when goods are bought for re-sale. If stock is sold for cash then it becomes cash or bank. If it's a credit transaction then stock becomes debtors. When debtors pay they become cash or bank.

So the business is able to make **profit** by changing stock into cash, bank or debtors at selling price, having bought it at cost price.

Please note that the stock figure on the balance sheet is always the **closing stock** since it's the balance of stock at the balance sheet date.

Capital is the value of what the owner contributed to the business. It could be in cash form or the actual business requirements like furniture. If its cash then it's used to pay for requirements which include machines, equipment, furniture, stock, labour, and others. However, capital can also be borrowed.

Net Profit appears on the balance sheet because it's the reward to the owner and it's added to capital. If it's a net loss then it's deducted.

Drawings appear on the balance sheet because it reduces capital. The business belongs to the owner and they are free to take cash or goods for their personal use. However, whenever they take drawings it reduces their investment. So drawings are taken with some precaution. If capital is to grow, drawings should be less than the profit made.

Owner's Equity is the capital which belongs to the owner. It's got by adding net profit to opening capital, and deducting drawings.

Borrowed Capital is the money used in a business but doesn't belong to the owner. It's borrowed from the bank or other financial institutions and is repaid over several years. It is referred to as long term liabilities.

Capital Employed is the total amount of capital used in a business. It's got by adding the **owner's equity** to **borrowed capital.**

Liabilities is money which the business owes to individuals, businesses or other institutions. If a business doesn't have liabilities then its assets are wholly financed by the owner's equity. We have current liabilities and long term liabilities.

Long Term Liabilities is money borrowed by the business and its period of repayment is beyond 12 months. It includes loans from banks or other financial institutions. **A loan** is money borrowed from a bank and the period of repayment could be between one and five years.

Current liabilities is borrowed money, or goods bought on credit and payment is made within 12 months. Examples are creditors and bank overdraft. Stock bought on credit creates creditors.

An injection is extra capital contributed by the owner during the year. It can be in cash form or some other assets. An injection is reflected on the balance sheet as an addition to opening capital.

6.2   The Accounting Equation

The accounting equation is a formula which explains the relationship between assets, capital and liabilities. It's also known as the **balance sheet equation** because it's the same items that we find on a balance sheet. The equation or formula is;

$$A \ = \ C + L$$
$$\textbf{Assets} \ = \ \textbf{Capital + Liabilities};$$

Assets are made up of fixed assets and current assets, whereas liabilities are made up of long term liabilities and current liabilities. So the above formula can be re-presented as;

$$\textbf{FA + CA = C + LTL + CL}$$

Fixed Assets + Current Assets = Capital + Long Term Liabilities + Current Liabilities.

Capital is contributed and belongs to the owner, not to the business. Therefore, capital is also a **liability** to the business. What belongs to the business are the assets. They are acquired using capital and liabilities which don't belong to the business. Therefore, what is owned is equal to what is owed. Basing on this assumption, we have the formula;

$$A = L ; \quad \textbf{Assets = Liabilities;} \quad \text{being true.}$$

Therefore, the layout of the balance sheet is based on the accounting equation and that's why it balances.

6.3   The Accounting Equation Format

This is the layout followed when preparing a balance sheet. The horizontal format is being abandoned for the more modern vertical format that is also used by computer programs. One of the vertical balance sheet formats is based exactly on the accounting equation of;

$$A = C + L \quad \textbf{Assets = Capital + Liabilities}$$

This means that all assets were bought using capital plus liabilities. If the business doesn't have liabilities then all assets were bought using capital provided by the owner. So the assets are equal to capital in that case.

Note: The **capital** referred to in the formulae is after net profit is added and drawings are deducted

This balance sheet format based on the accounting equation is illustrated below:

Jackson's Balance Sheet as at 31st December 2006		
The Assets Section		
Fixed Asstes		
Land and buildings		50,000
Motor vehicles		20,910
Furniture and fittings		+ 7,000
Total Fixed Assets		77,910
Current Assets		
Stock	17,600	
Debtors	11,563	
Cash	+ 790	
Total Current Assets		+ 29,953
Total Assets		**107,863**
The Liabilities Section		
Capital at start		94,380
add Net Profit		24,141
		118,521
less Drawings		27,495
Owner's Equity		91,026
Long Term Liabilities		
Bank Loan		2,100
Current Liabilities		
Creditors	4,737	
Bank overdraft	+10,000	
Total Current Liabilities		+ 14,737
Total Liabilities		**107,863**

In the upper section we start with fixed assets since they stay longer than current assets. Fixed Assets are arranged according to the **order of permanency**. This is where the most permanent asset is recorded first and the least permanent is recorded last. **Permanency** refers to how long the asset is expected to be used. A particular building can be used for 15 years but some furniture can only last 2 years.

Current assets are recorded in the **order of liquidity**. This is where we start with the most difficult to turn into cash, and end with cash that is already liquid, in notes and coins. Stock is the most difficult since it may first be sold on credit before the debtors can pay. Bank is turned into cash by just withdrawing it. So its stock first, then debtors, bank, and finally cash itself.

We add total fixed assets to total current assets to get **Total Assets.**

The totals for the **assets section** and the **liabilities section** are supposed to be the same and that is when the balance sheet is said to have **balanced.** If the two are not the same then there are some errors.

In the lower section (the liability section), we start with **capital** which stays as long as the business is operational. We add net profit and deduct drawings to get the new **owner's equity.** A **net loss** is deducted. We then record long term liabilities and lastly the current liabilities with the bigger values first. Adding the owner's equity to long term and current liabilities gives us a total that is equal to total assets in the upper section. This is the test for **accuracy** on the balance sheet and the other records compiled earlier.

From the basic accounting equation of **A = C + L,** we get the following formulae by substitution;

1.   **Capital = Assets - Liabilities**   C = A - L;

2.   **Liabilities = Assets - Capital**   L = A - C

You can use these formulae to derive some figures which are not provided in an exercise.

EXERCISE 6A.

Using the accounting equation, complete the following table by filling in the missing amounts.

	Assets	Liabilities	Capital
I	11,000	2,450	....
II	35,000	7,500	....
III	22,500	....	20,000
IV	....	500	14,700
V	19,250	725	....
VI	27,270	....	26,120
VII	....	375	15,745
VIII	9,775	155	....
IX	2,719	....	2,502
X	....	1,200	18,799

EXERCISE 6B.

Compile a balance sheet using the equation; A = C + L, from the following figures;   Capital 35,600   Cash   350
Stock   1,200   Bank   6,250   Motor   vehicles 21,000
Creditors 700   Office equipment 7,500

6.4   The Net Assets Format

The second balance sheet format is based on the **Net Assets** formula which is;

$$NA = C + LTL$$

Net Assets = Capital + Long Term Liabilities

$$NA = FA + CA - CL$$

Net Assets = Fixed Assets + Current Assets - Current Liabilities.

To get this formula, we shifted current liabilities on the accounting equation, from the liabilities side to the asset's side, by deducting it from both.

$$C + LTL + CL - CL, \text{ which leaves only } C + LTL$$

When we deduct current liabilities from the assets we are left with net assets and the name for the section changes to net asset's.

This balance sheet format is illustrated below;

Jackson's Balance Sheet as at 31st December 2006		
Net Assets Section		
Fixed Assets		
Land and Buildings		50,000
Motor vehicles		20,910
Furniture and Fittings		+ 7,000
Total Fixed Assets		77,910
Current Assets		
Stock	17,600	
Debtors	11,563	
Cash	+ 790	
Total Current Assets	29,953	
Current Liabilities		
Bank Overdraft	10,000	
Creditors	+ 4,737	
Total Current Liabilities	- 14,737	
Net Current Assets		+ 15,216
Net Assets		**93,126**
Capital Employed Section		
Capital at start		94,380
Net Profit		+ 24,141
		118,521
Drawings		- 27,495
Owner's Equity		91,026
Long Term Liabilities		
Bank Loan		+ 2,100
Capital Employed		**93,126**

From this balance sheet we can prove the following formulae;

NA   **=**   **C + LTL**

$93,126 = 91,026 + 2,100$

NA   **=**   **FA +**   **CA -**   **CL =**   **A - CL**

$93,126 = 77,910 + 29,953 - 14,737 = 107,863 - 14,737$

CA - CL   **= NCA** (Net Current Assets)

$29,953 - 14,737 = 15,216$

Therefore, **NA =**   **FA + NCA**

$93,126 = 77,910 + 15,216$

From the above formulae we can conclude that;

NA = FA + NCA = C + LTL

If we split NCA then the formula becomes;

NA   **=**   **FA +**   **CA -**   **CL =**   **C + LTL**

$93,126 = 77,910 + 29,953 - 14,737 = 91,026 + 2,100$

In the **Net Assets section,** we start with fixed assets in order of permanency, followed by current assets in order of liquidity, and end with current liabilities in order of value. We **deduct** Total Current Liabilities (**TCL**) from Total Current Assets (**TCA**) to get Net Current Assets (**NCA**) if the answer is positive. If the answer is negative then its **Net Current Liabilities** (**NCL**). Net current assets / liabilities is **added** to total fixed assets (**TFA**) to get Net Assets (**NA**). Net Current Assets is commonly referred to as working capital.

In the **capital employed section** we start with capital, add net profit and deduct drawings to get the new owner's equity. If it was a **net loss** then it's deducted from opening capital. We then **add** long term liabilities to get the capital employed. **Capital Employed (CE)** is the total capital used in the business. It's made up of owner's equity and borrowed capital in form of long term liabilities. If the business doesn't have any long term liabilities then the capital invested by the owner is the same as the capital employed. Therefore, the capital employed figure should be **equal** to the net assets figure.

Note: Because of the need and importance to show working capital on the balance sheet, most people use the **Net Assets format** and we shall stick to that.

EXERCISE 6C.

Prepare a balance sheet using the formula; NA = C + LTL, from the following figures as at 31st May 2004.

Land and buildings	40,000	Net Profit	8,700
Furniture and fittings	6,000	Bank overdraft	550
Stock	780	Creditors	1,170
Debtors	4,500	Cash	700
Drawings	850	Capital	42,410

EXERCISE 6D.

*Can you group the following into **current assets, fixed assets, long term liabilities,** and **current liabilities;**   Bank overdraft, Debtors, Creditors, Land and buildings, stock, Bank loan, Office equipment, cash, furniture and fittings, Bank, Motor vehicles.*

6.5   Balance Sheet Errors

A balance sheet is supposed to **balance** by having the two totals being the same. If it doesn't balance then there are some errors which need to be identified and corrected before it can balance. Having compiled a trial balance and it balanced prior on. The problems affecting the balancing should be on the balance sheet itself, or the trading, profit and loss account. They should be solved by the following procedure. You should only proceed to the next step if a particular step doesn't solve the problem.

i)   **Re-add** all the figures and **sub totals** on the balance sheet to ensure it was done properly.

ii)   Ensure that all the assets, liabilities, capital, net profit, and drawings were **all recorded** on the balance sheet, and are in the right places.

iii)   The next step is to **thoroughly** check the **additions** and **subtractions** on the trading, profit and loss account. The errors discovered here have an effect on net profit. If net profit changes then we should make adjustments on the balance sheet and probably have the problem solved.

iv)   The final step should ensure that the **contents of the trading profit and loss account** are the right ones and are in the right place. Ensure that all incomes and expenses are there. Any effect on net profit should be corrected on the balance sheet as well.

This final step should enable the balance sheet to balance.

6.6   The Importance Of A Balance Sheet

1. It's a summary statement which shows the financial position of a business.

2. It shows what the business owns in terms of fixed and current assets, and what it owes in form of current and long-term liabilities.

3. When it balances it helps to prove that recording was done properly and there is mathematical accuracy up to the final accounts.

Multiple Choice and Short Answer Questions

1. The formula for net current assets is:

A. Fixed assets - Current liabilities.   B. Fixed assets + Current assets.

C   Capital +current liabilities

D. Current assets - current liabilities.

2.   The best definition for a balance sheet is:

A list of assets, liabilities and capital   B. A list of all assets.

C   A list of assets and capital   D. A list of all accounts

3.   On the balance sheet, net profit is

A. Deducted from business assets.   B. Added to capital.

C. Added to current liabilities.   D. Deducted from capital.

4.   Capital employed is equal to

A.   Capital + net profit - drawings.

B.   Capital + net profit + drawings - long term liabilities.

C.   Capital + net profit - drawings + long term liabilities.

D.   Capital + long term liabilities - net profit-drawings

5.   Current assets less current liabilities is the formula for

A. Working capital   B. Net assets

C. Current ratio   D. Capital

6.   Which of the following is a long term liability?

A. Creditors   B. Overdraft   C. Loan   D. Debtors

7.   Which of the following is a current asset?

A.   Debtors   B. Creditors   C. Motor vehicle   D. Furniture

8. Which of the following is a liability?

A. Overdraft   B. Stock   C. Cash   D. Debtors

9.   Explain the following;

[a] Balance sheet   [b] capital employed   [c] net assets

10.   Differentiate between the following;

[a] Fixed assets and current assets

[b] long-term liabilities and current liabilities

[c] owners equity and borrowed capital

[e] net current assets and net current liabilities

EXERCISE 6E.

On 30th June 2006, Christine extracted the following balances from her books. Closing stock was 12,850.

Capital	12,022	Cash in hand	20
Wages	6,121	Sundry Expenses	312
Electricity	80	Insurance	219
Discount Allowed	420	Salaries	1,000
Stock at 1st July 2005	9,645	Purchases	29,781
Repairs	158	Creditors	8,165
Sales	37,730	Debtors	9,036
Bank overdraft	739	Rent and rates	1,500
		Travelling Expenses	364

Required: (a) A trial balance at 30th June 2006.
(b) A trading, profit and loss account for the year to 30th June 2006.
(c) A balance sheet at 30th June 2009.

EXERCISE 6F.

Taylor started his business for the month of September 2003 with cash $2,100, Bank $55,000 and Stock $765

2nd   Bought a motor vehicle at $37,500 by cheque.
2nd   Purchased stock for re-sale at $14,750 by cheque.
3rd   Paid for furniture and fittings at $4,300 by cheque.
4th   Received a cheque for sales at $6,500
6th   Bought equipment by cheque at $5,200
8th   Paid advertising expense by cash $235
9th   Purchased stationery at $180 cash
12th Paid insurance premium at $120 cash
13th Sold unwanted chair at $1,200 cash
14th Sold goods for $8,200 by cheque
16th Paid electricity bill of $175 cash
19th Received a cheque for goods sold at $4,150
20th Drew cash for personal use $1,450
23rd Bought more stock at $6,500 by cheque.
27th   Received rent by cash $1,400
30th Sent a cheque to the land lord for rent of $1,800
His closing stock was $8,240.

You are required to write his cashbook, post to the ledger, extract a trial balance, compile a trading account,
profit and loss account and Balance sheet. You should show closing transfers on income and expense accounts.

ANSWERS

<u>6A</u>

I	8,550	II	27,500	III	2,500	IV	15,200
V	18,525	VI	1,150	VII	16,120	VIII	9,620
IX	217	X	19,999				

<u>6B</u>

Balance Sheet

Assets Section		
Fixed Assets		
Motor vehicles		21,000
Office equipment		7,500
TFA		28,500
Current Assets		
Stock	1,200	
Bank	6,250	
Cash	350	
TCA		7,800
		36,300
Liabilities Section		
Capital		35,600
Current Liabilities		
Creditors		700
Total Liabilities		**36,300**

SUBSIDIARY BOOKS AND CREDIT

7.1   Subsidiary Books

A **subsidiary book** is a book of accounts where transactions are first recorded before posting to the ledger. Small businesses normally operate on a cash basis whereas the big ones have many of their transactions on credit. In order to **reduce the number of transactions** in the ledger, subsidiary books were introduced for recording the detail of transactions. It's only totals that are posted to the general ledger.

The introduction of subsidiary books also aimed at **dividing up the work**. The large number of transactions can be recorded by different people, in different books, at the same time. So a large amount of work is done in a shorter period and time is saved.

The different types of subsidiary books are illustrated below.

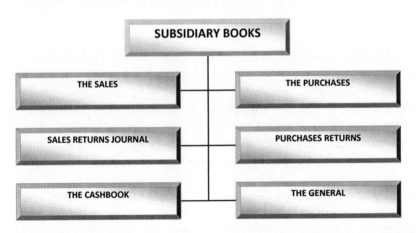

Subsidiary books are also known as **books of original entry, or books of prime entry**. However, subsidiary books are **not** part of the double entry system. They are only designed **to assist** the ledger by handling the detail of recording.

The Cashbook is a subsidiary book where **cash transactions** are first recorded before being posted to the ledger. We learnt in chapter 3 that the cashbook is part of the ledger. Therefore, the cashbook is both a subsidiary book and a section of the ledger.

The Purchases Journal is a subsidiary book where **credit purchases** are first recorded before posting to the ledger.

The Sales Journal is a subsidiary book where credit **sales** are first recorded before they are posted to the ledger.

The sales returns journal and the purchases returns journal are explained in chapter 8, while the general journal is in chapter 9.

A debtor is an individual, institution, or business that bought on credit.

A creditor is a person or business from which the business bought on credit.

A debtor owes the business while a creditor is owed by the business.

The sales journal and purchases journal are both recorded in a **journal book** whose columns are illustrated below;

Date	Details	Folio	Debit	Credit

Below is an explanation of how we use the columns;
 ♦ The details column is where we write the name of the account where the amount is to be posted
 ♦ The folio column is where we write the ledger section and account number where the transaction is posted.
 ♦ The debit column is where we write the amount to be debited
 ♦ The credit column is where we write the amount to be credited

At the real place of work we have separate books for each subsidiary book. However, for learning purposes we have one journal book that we use for all the different Journals. So we write and complete one type of journal before we proceed to the next journal for the same exercise.

7.2   Credit Transactions

A credit transaction is where a service or good is passed on to a buyer before full payment is made. The business buys and sells stock on credit, and that is the main focus of this chapter.

When a credit transaction takes place, the document prepared is **an invoice.**

The recording of assets and services bought on credit is explained in section 9.5.

You may not find the word **"credit"** in some transactions yet they are. Therefore, any transaction where you find the supplier or buyer's **name** with no mention of payment, it should be treated as a credit transaction. For **cash transactions**, there is always mention of cash or a cheque.

7.3   The Purchases Journal

The Purchases Journal is a subsidiary book where credit purchases are first recorded before they are posted.

Credit purchases are goods bought for re-sale and full payment is only made later. The business receives an invoice which we refer to as a **purchases invoice,** and the seller becomes a **creditor.** This **invoice received** is the source of information recorded in the purchases journal.

Cash purchases is where full payment is made before the business receives the stock.

The purchases journal is used for listing and getting the total of credit purchases. Recording in the purchases journal is based on **double entry.** The individual value of purchases invoices are recorded in the credit column, while their total is recorded in the debit column. We start by recording individual invoices, the date, the supplier's name in the details column, and the amount in the credit column. They are recorded in order of date until we get to the last credit purchase for the month. We then get their total and record it in the debit column. In the details column against this total, we write; **'debit purchases account',** since that's where it's to be debited.

Below are some transactions and the purchases journal to illustrate this;
Nov.1st Received an invoice from Stewart for $250
5th Bought goods on credit from Linda at $320
8th An invoice for $110 was received from Newton

Date	Details	Debit	Credit
	Jackson's Purchases Journal for November 2005		
1	Stewart		250
5	Linda		320
8	Newton		110
30	**Debit Purchases Account**	680	

The heading for the purchases journal should indicate the name of the business and the month for which it's written.

We can conclude that; the purchases journal is just a list of credit purchases showing the date, the supplier, the amount, and the total of credit purchases for the period.

EXERCISE 7A. Record the following transactions in the Purchases Journal for Marcos General Dealers for the month of March 2005.
2nd   Bought goods on credit from Walker for $321.50.
7th   Purchased stock on credit from Belinda for $115.20
12th   Bought stock from Ceaser for $87.30
17th   Purchased goods for re-sale from Agatha at $74.10
25th   More stock was bought from Walker at $100

7.4   The Sales Journal

The sales journal is a subsidiary book where credit sales are first recorded before they are posted. It's used for listing and getting the total of credit sales.

An invoice is given or **sent** to the buyer and it's referred to as a **sales invoice**. The customer who bought on credit becomes **a debtor**. The copy which remains in the invoice book is what we use as source document for recording the **sales journal.**

Below are some transactions and a sales journal ;
Nov.   3rd   Sent an invoice to Nadia for $175
        7th   Sold goods on credit to Kate for $310
        12th   Sent an invoice to Timothy for $100
The above transactions are recorded in the sales journal as follows;

Date	Details	Dr	Cr
	Jackson's Sales Journal for November 2005		
3	Nadiya	175	
7	Kate	310	
12	Timothy	100	
30	**Credit Sales Account**		585

We write the date, the debtor's name in the details column, and the amount in the debit column since they are the receiver. This is done for all credit sales made during the month. Their total is recorded in the credit column and we write; **"Credit Sales Account"** in the details column. This is the instruction followed when posting to the ledger.

The heading for the sales journal indicates the name of the business and the month for which it's written, as illustrated above.

We can conclude that; the sales journal is just a list of credit sales showing the date, the name of debtors, the amount, and the total of credit sales for the period.

EXERCISE 7B.
Write a Sales Journal for Tamara for June 2004
1st   Melvin bought goods on credit valued at $45.50
6th   Sold goods on credit to Rhoda for $127.30
14th   Kenneth bought stock for $67.70
19th   Stock sold to Melvin for $90.00
28th   Sold goods to Henrietta for $82.80

7.5   Posting The Purchases Journal

The recording of transactions in subsidiary books is not part of double entry, except for those recorded in the cashbook, that is part of the ledger.

Posting is the recording of transactions in the ledger after their initial entry in a subsidiary book. Before posting we open an account for each creditor. **All transactions** involving a particular creditor are recorded on that creditor's single account. We also open a purchases account if it's not yet open.

When posting, the amount in the **credit column** is **credited** to the creditor whose name is written in the details column. This is done for all figures in the credit column. The total in the **debit column** is **debited** to the purchases account.

According to the purchases journal on the previous pages;
♦   the Stewart account is credited with $250,
♦   the Linda account is credited with $320,
♦   the Newton account is credited with $110. and
♦   the purchases account is debited with the total of $680

as illustrated below;

Stewart Account

			1	Purchases	PJ	250

Linda Account

			5	Purchases	PJ	320

Newton Account

			8	Purchases	PJ	110

Purchases Account

	Cash or Bank	CB	315	30	To Trading Account	995
30	Creditors	PJ	680			
			995			995

All the credit entries have **one single corresponding debit entry** on the purchases account and that is their total. The purchases journal reduces the many credit purchases to just a single entry on the purchases account at the end of the month.

For all the credit entries we write **purchases** in their details column because, that is where their corresponding, single debit entry is recorded. On the purchases account we write **creditors** since the corresponding entries for the total are found on the different creditor's accounts.

Credit purchases are recorded on the **same account with cash purchases**. The corresponding entry for cash purchases is in the cashbook. The only difference is that cash purchases are posted individually and probably daily. Credit purchases are only posted at month end after totalling up and they appear last on the account.

Note: If goods are bought from a supplier and it's a cash transaction, we don't need to open an account for them. We simply debit purchases and credit the cashbook.

7.6   Posting The Sales Journal

Before posting any transactions, we open accounts for each debtor, plus the sales account if it's not yet open.

When posting, the amount in the debit column is **debited** to the debtor's account whose name appears in the details column. The total in the credit column is **credited** to the sales account

According to the sales journal on the previous pages,   we;

♦   debit the Nadia account with $175,

♦   debit the Kate Account with $310

♦   debit the Timothy Account with $100, and

♦   credit the Sales Account with the total of $585 as illustrated below;

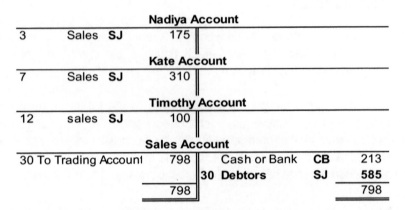

Nadiya Account

3	Sales **SJ**	175

Kate Account

7	Sales **SJ**	310

Timothy Account

12	sales **SJ**	100

Sales Account

30 To Trading Account	798	Cash or Bank	**CB**	213
		30 Debtors	**SJ**	**585**
	798			798

For all the entries on the debtor's accounts, we write **sales** in the details column. That is where their single corresponding credit entry is found. In the details column on the sales account we write **debtors.** That is where its corresponding entries are found, on the different debtor's accounts.

Credit sales are recorded on the **same account as cash sales** as illustrated above. The corresponding entry for cash sales is in the cashbook. The only difference is that cash sales are posted individually and probably daily, whereas credit sales are only posted as a total at month end. So they appear last on the account.

Note: We don't open accounts for customers who pay cash or by cheque because they are cash transactions.

EXERCISE 7C.
Complete the purchases journal and sales journal for Bob's Spares.
Post them to the ledger at the end of October 2001.
4th   Purchased stock from Polly for $47.20
5th   Sold goods on credit to Patrick for $25.00
9th   Bought goods from Raymond for $61.90
11th   Sales were made to Daniel for $43.40
13th   Purchases goods from Lorna for $84.50
15th   Stock was sold to Mandela for $55.20

19th   More stock was bought from Raymond for $75.80
20th   More sales were made to Daniel for $70.75
23rd   Bought stock from Mamba valued at $96.30
24th   Patrick bought more goods for $75.30
27th   More goods were bought from Lorna for $59.70
28th   Goods were sold to Naomi for $24.20
30th   Solome bought stock for $30.35

7.7   Folio Columns

The folio columns in the purchases journal and sales journal are only filled in after the posting is done. That's when we know the account numbers where the amount is posted. Therefore, each figure in the purchases journal and sales journal should have a folio number entered after it's been posted.

For all postings from the purchases journal, we write **PJ** in the **folio column** meaning purchases journal as illustrated on page 68. We don't write the account number of the corresponding entry because there is none. All we have are the individual amounts credited and their total debited. The only book where you can get details is the purchases journal.

For all postings from the sales journal to the ledger, we write **SJ** in the folio column meaning sales journal as illustrated on page 68.

7.8   Payment To Creditors

Before a buyer can take goods on credit, the seller should be satisfied they will pay. When a debtor pays or creditor is paid, the cashbook is the subsidiary book.

For cash payments a receipt is received and it serves as the source document. For cheque payments, we use the **cheque stub** as the source document. When a creditor is paid, we credit the cashbook- **as giver** and debit the creditor- **as receiver.**

This is illustrated using the following payments;
14th   Paid Stewart $100 by cheque
17th   Paid Linda $250 by cheque
24th   Paid Newton $60 by cash

Below is their recording in the cashbook;

Dr side				Cr side of Cashbook	
Cash	Bank	Date	Payments	Cash	Bank
		14	Stewart		100
		17	Linda		250
		24	Newton	60	

We write the creditor's name in the payments column.
The above cashbook is posted to the ledger as illustrated below;

CREDITOR'S ACCOUNTS

Stewart Account

14	Bank	100	1	Purchases	250
30	Balance c/d	150			
		250			250
			1	Balance b/d	150

Linda Account

17	Bank	250	5	Purchases	320
30	Balance c/d	70			
		320			320
			1	Balance b/d	70

Newton Account

24	Cash	60	8	Purchases	110
30	Balance c/d	50			
		110			110
			1	Balance b/d	50

We write cash or bank in the details column, depending on how it was paid.

So each creditor's account is debited with what is paid to them, and credited with credit purchases. Each account is balanced to get the outstanding amount at the period end.

7.9   Receipts From Debtors

When a debtor pays we credit their account - **as giver**, and debit the cashbook - **as receiver**. The source document for cash received is the receipt copy retained. Although a receipt is written for cheques, we either use the cheque or deposit slip as source document.
This is illustrated using the following receipts;
11th Received cheque from Nadia for $120,
18th Kate paid $210 by cheque,
21st Timothy paid $75 in cash.

Below is their recording in the cashbook;

Dr side							Cr side	
Date	Receipts	Fo	DA	Cash	Bank	Date	Payments	
11	Nadia				120			
18	Kate				210			
21	Timothy			75				

Header: **CASH BOOK**

These entries are posted to the ledger as illustrated below;

DEBTOR'S ACCOUNTS

Nadia Account

3	Sales	175	11	Bank	120
			30	Balance c/d	55
		175			175
1	Balance b/d	55			

Kate Account

7	Sales	310	18	Bank	210
			30	Balance c/d	100
		310			310
1	Balance b/d	100			

Timothy Account

12	Sales	100	21	Cash	75
			30	Balance c/d	25
		100			100
1	Balance b/d	25			

We write cash or bank in the details column, depending on how it was paid.

So each debtor's account is debited with credit sales and credited with what they pay. Each account is balanced to get the outstanding amount at the period end.

Please note: Transactions should always be recorded in the order of date, first transactions first.

EXERCISE 7D.

Prepare a Purchases Journal, Sales Journal, and Cashbook for Kelvin's Green Grocer and post them to the ledger at the end of November 2001. Remember to extract a Trial Balance.

1st Started business with $450 cash and a bank balance of $2,900
1st Purchased furniture using a cheque for $750
2nd Bought stock on credit from Regina for $1,400
3rd Purchased stationery using cash $35
4th Sold goods to Grant for $730

5th   Sold stock for cash $320
8th   Paid advertising expenses by cash $120
9th   Goods sold to Banda for $420
10th   Purchases were made from Thomas for $1,350
13th   Paid Regina $1,250 by cheque
15th   Sales were made to Miranda for $650
18th   Bought stock from Alva for $1,600
20th   Paid for the business license by cheque $270
22nd   Miranda paid $245 by cash
24th   Sold stock to Craig for $970
26th   Paid Thomas $650 by cheque
29th   Received a cheque of $850 from Craig
30th   Paid wages $450 using cash

Multiple Choice and Short Answer Questions

1.   Which one of the following is not another term for a journal?
A   Subsidiary book   B. Book of prime entry
C.   Ledger book   D. Book of first entry
2.   The total of the purchases journal is posted to the
A   Debit side of the purchases day book
B. Credit side of the purchases day book
C. Debit side of the purchases account
D. Credit side of the purchases account
3.   The sales journal is posted to the ledger by:
A   Debiting sales account and crediting debtor's account
B   Crediting sales account and debiting debtors accounts
C. Crediting ledger account and debiting sales
D.   None of the above
4.   The source document for credit sales is an
A   invoice sent   B. invoice received
C. cashbook   D. purchases
5.   The subsidiary book for credit purchases is
A   general journal   B. sales journal
C. cashbook   D. purchases journal
6. Cash received from debtors is first recorded in the.............................
7. The source document for the purchases daybook is the ....
8. The subsidiary book posted to the sales account and the debtor's account is the ....
9. Explain the process of recording transactions in the sales journal and purchases journal.
10. How do you post the purchases journal and sales journal to the ledger?
11. Explain the process of recording;   [a] payments to creditors
                                            [b] receipts from debtors.
12. Name and explain the use of each of the different subsidiary books.

EXERCISE 7E.

The following transactions were extracted from Parker's books for the month of January 2007. He started the period with cash 450 and 2,350 at the bank. His opening stock was $325 and closing stock was $1,350. Prepare his subsidiary books, post to the ledger, extract a trial balance and write his trading, profit and loss account.

1st   Bought Furniture by cheque for 1,140
2nd   Purchased stock for re-sale at 350 by cheque
2nd   Used cash to buy stationary for 41
3rd   Made sales for cash 222
4th   Bought stock from Patricia for 580
5th   Sold goods to Martin for 435
5th   Paid for small expenses by cash 23
7th   Paid Patricia by cheque 580
9th   Stock was sold to Rodney for 720
10th   Earned a commission of 180 by cash
12th   Paid cash for advertising expenses 140
13th   Purchased stock from Nana for 670
14th   Received a cheque from Martin for 240
16th   Received a cheque for cash sales 1,200
19th   Stock was bought from Simon for 925
20th   Rodney paid by cheque 420
23rd   More goods were bought from Patricia for 810
24th   Made credit sales to Sally for 384
25th   Paid cash for repairs at 37
26th   Sent a cheque to Nana for 650
27th   Paid Simon 430 by cheque
28th   Cleared the wages bill of 470 using cash
28th   Sold goods for a cheque of 735.
29th   More sales were made to Martin for 880
30th   Sent a cheque of 1,500 to the Landlord for rent

ANSWERS

7A

Purchases Journal for March 1995

Mar-02	Walker		321.50
7	Belinda		115.20
12	Ceasar		87.30
17	Agatha		74.10
25	Walker		100.00
Debit Purchase a/c		698.10	

7B

Sales Journal for June 1984

1	Melvin	45.50	
6	Rhoda	127.30	
14	Kenneth	67.70	
19	Melvin	90.00	
28	Henrietta	82.80	
Credit Sales a/c			413.30

RETURNS

8.1   Returns

Returns are goods returned by the buyer because they are **unsatisfactory**. Goods are unsatisfactory if they;

i)   are **not the right ones ordered**,
ii)   have a **fault**,
iii)   are **poor quality**
iv)   were **damaged** in transit,
v)   are **more than the quantity ordered**.

Goods returned into the business are referred to as **returns inwards**. They were sales before being returned and that is why they are referred to as **sales returns**.

Goods returned to suppliers or creditors are **returns outwards**. They were purchases before being returned and that's why they are referred to as **purchases returns**.

For a cash sale, cash is received immediately. We debit the cashbook and credit the sales account. Returns for a cash sale are refunded immediately across the counter. The subsidiary book is the cashbook which is credited, while the debit entry is on the sales account, or sale returns account.

If it was a cash purchase and they are returned then a refund is received immediately. The subsidiary book is the cashbook which is debited while the credit entry is on the purchases account, or the purchases returns account.

For credit transactions the refund is not immediate since the goods are not yet paid for. We just adjust the accounts to reduce the debt and this is done by initial recording in the purchases returns journal, and the sales returns journal.

8.2 Purchases Returns Journal

The Purchases Returns Journal is a subsidiary book where **purchases returns** are first recorded before being posted to the ledger. It's also called the **returns outwards journal**.

When recording we start with the date. In the **details column** we write the creditor who received the returned goods. The value of goods is entered in the **debit column** since the creditor is the receiver. We record all the other returns for the month using the same procedure. At month end we find a total for all the figures in the debit column and record it in the credit column. In the details column against the total we write, **"Credit purchases returns account"**. This means that when posting, the credit entry is made on the purchases returns account.

Below is an illustration of transactions and their recording;
4th   Returned goods to Stewart for $12
9th   Stock for $20 was returned to Linda
13th   Goods were returned to Newton for $15

Date	Details	Folio	Dr	Cr
	Purchases Returns Journal			
4	Stewart		12	
9	Linda		20	
13	Newton		15	
30	Credit Purchases Returns A/c			47

Entries in this journal follow double entry. The figures are in the debit column and re-appear in the credit column as part of the total.

When purchases are returned to a creditor, a **debit note** is written which goes with the goods. Normally the creditor sends a **credit note** in response, to acknowledge they received the goods. The **source of information** for entry in the purchases returns journal is either the credit note received or the debit note sent. (Explained in 8.6 and 8.7)

EXERCISE 8A.
Write the following transactions in a purchases returns journal
6th   Returned goods to Yvonne for $36
11th   Stock for $23 was returned to Fortune
17th   Goods were returned to Malcolm for $40
22nd   Returned stock to Cyprian for $17

8.3   Sales Returns Journal

The Sales Returns Journal is a subsidiary book where **sales returns** are first recorded before posting to the ledger. It's also called the **returns inwards journal**.

When recording we start with the date. In the **details column** we write the debtor who returned goods. The value of goods is entered in the **credit column** since they are the giver. We record all the other returns for the month using same procedure. At month end we find a total for all the figures in the credit column and record it in the debit column. In the details column against the total we write, **"Debit sales returns account"**. This means that when posting, the debit entry is made on the sales returns account.

Below is an illustration of transactions and their recording;
6th Nadia returned goods for $30
10th Sales were returned by Kate for $25
16th Timothy returned unsatisfactory goods for $18

Date	Details	Folio	Dr	Cr
	Sales Returns Journal			
6	Nadia			30
10	Kate			25
16	Timothy			18
30	Debit Sales Returns a/c		73	

Entries in this journal also follow the double entry.
When sales are returned they are normally accompanied with a **debit note** from the debtor. In response the business issues a **credit note** as an acknowledgement of receipt of goods returned. The **source document** for recording the sales returns journal is either the credit note sent or a debit note received. (Section 8.6 & 8.7)

EXERCISE 8B.
Compile a sales returns journal from the following;
8th Sidney returned goods for $29
14th Sales were returned by Victor for $42
19th Norah returned unsatisfactory goods for $38
25th Timothy returned goods for $25

8.4   Posting Purchases Returns Journals

The purchases returns journal is posted like other journals. The amount in the debit column is posted to the debit side of the account written in the details column. According to the purchases returns journal on page 78, $12 is debited to the Stewart account, $20 is debited to the Linda account, and $15 is debited to the Newton account. The corresponding credit entry is for the **total amount** that is credited to the purchases returns account. Below are the ledger accounts illustrated;

Stewart Account

4	Purchases Returns	12	1	Purchases		250
14	Bank	100				
30	Balance c/d	138				
		250				250
			1	Balance b/d		138

Linda Account

9	Returns	20	5	Purchases		320
17	Bank	250				
30	Balance c/d	50				
		320				320
			1	Balance b/d		50

Newton Account

13	Returns	15	8	Purchases		110
24	Cash	60				
30	Balance c/d	35				
		110				110
			1	Balance b/d		35

Purchases Returns Account

30	To Trading Account	47	30	Creditors	47

Note that previous entries regarding these particular creditors are included, and the accounts are balanced to give a better picture.

For each of the debit entries on the creditor's accounts we write **'Purchases Returns'** in the details column. That's because the corresponding entry is found there. We may shorten it to **'Returns'**

For their **corresponding credit entry** on the purchases returns account we write **'creditors'**. This is because the corresponding entries are found on creditor's accounts.

However, in the absence of the purchases returns account, these returns are credited to the purchases account. So the amount transferred to the trading account is **net purchases** since returns are deducted in the balancing process.

The purchases returns account has a credit balance and it's recorded among the credit balances on the **trial balance**.

8.5   Posting Sales Returns Journal

The amount in the credit column is posted to the credit side of the account written in the details column. According to the sales returns journal on page 79, $30 is credited to the Nadia account, $25 is credited to the Kate account, and $18 is credited to the Timothy account as illustrated below;

Nadia Account

3	Sales	175	6	Returns	30
			11	Bank	120
			30	Balance c/d	25
		175			175
1	Balance b/d	25			

Kate Account

7	Sales	310	10	Sales Returns	25
			18	Bank	210
			30	Balance c/d	75
		310			310
1	Balance b/d	75			

Timothy Account

12	Sales	100	16	Sales Returns	18
			21	Cash	75
			30	Balance c/d	7
		100			100
1	Balance b/d	7			

Sales Returns Account

30	Debtors	73	30	To Trading Account	73

Please note that previous entries regarding these debtors are included and their accounts are balanced to give a better picture.

For each of the credit entries on the debtor's accounts we write **'sales returns'** in the details column. That's because the corresponding entry is found there. We may shorten it to **'Returns'**.

Their **corresponding debit entry** is the total of $73 which is debited to the **sales returns account**. We write **'debtors'** in the details column because the corresponding entries are found on the debtor's accounts.

However, in the absence of the sales returns account, these returns are debited to the sales account. So, the amount transferred to the trading account is **net sales** since returns are deducted in the balancing process.

The sales returns account has a debit balance and it's recorded among debit balances on the **trial balance**.

8.6   A Credit Note

A **Credit Note** is a document **sent by a seller** to inform a buyer that their account is credited. Reasons for sending a credit note are;

♦   to **acknowledge receipt of goods returned** by a debtor.

♦   to correct an **over charge** to a debtor

♦   when giving an **allowance** to a debtor. (Explained in 8.8)

To differentiate it from other documents, it's normally printed in red since it reduces a debt, and yet most documents increase it.

Below is a sample, although it appears in black;

MFI SOLUTIONS, P.O.BOX 2134, RICHMOND						No.315	
TEL/FAX : 0208330779				Date...			
CREDIT NOTE				Delivery Note No..........			
TO : M/S...				Customer No...............			
Reason:...				Account No.....			
....				Invoice No...................			
Code	**Description**			**Unit**	**Qty.**	**Price**	**Disc.**	**Value**
						TOTAL	

A credit note sent has an effect of reducing what the debtor owes, and it's recorded in the **sales returns journal**. It's posted to the credit side of a debtor's account and this reduces the debt. The corresponding entry is made as part of the total in the sales returns journal. They are debited together to the sales returns account. Debiting this account reduces the sales value of on the income statement, as explained in 8.9.

The business **never receives** a credit note from a debtor. It receives credit notes from its creditors when;   it returns goods;
receives an allowance; or   has been over charged.

Credit notes received reduce what is owed and are recorded in the **purchases returns journal**. The total from the purchases returns journal reduces the value of purchases on the income statement as explained in 8.9.

A Credit note sent to a debtor is referred to as a **credit note sent**. The one received from a creditor is referred to as a **credit note received**.

An overcharge is an error where a buyer is charged more than what they should pay. An overcharge to a debtor is corrected by sending them a **credit note.** It reduces what they owe. If a business was over charged then a creditor sends a credit note to correct that. It's a credit note received.

8. 7   A Debit Note

A **Debit Note** is a document **sent by a seller or buyer,** to inform the receiver that their account is **debited** in the books of the sender. A debit note can be sent or received by a business.

A Debit Note sent to Debtors

A debit note is sent to a debtor when they had been undercharged.

An undercharge is an error where the buyer is charged less than what they should pay. It's corrected by sending a **debit note or another invoice** to the buyer. For example, if the business charged $50 to a buyer instead of $55. You correct this by sending another invoice, or debit note for $5.

The business also **sends** a debit note to a debtor if they fail to return **packaging containers** that were not part of the invoice. This increases what the debtor owes.

A debit note to a debtor is first recorded in the **sales journal**. It's then posted to the debit side of the debtor's account, and as part of the sales journal **total**, to the credit side of the sales account. The treatment and effect of this debit note is the same as that for a sales invoice.

Below is an illustration of a debit note;

MFI SOLUTIONS, P.O.BOX 2134, RICHMOND						No.222		
TEL/FAX : 0208330779								
DEBIT NOTE				Date........................				
				Delivery Note No.............				
TO : M/S..				Account No................				
Reason..				Invoice No..................				
....								
Code	Description		Unit	Qty.	Price	Disc.	Value	
					TOTAL			
Your account has been debited with the total amount shown.								

A Debit Note received from a Debtor

The business receives a debit note when a debtor returns goods or discovers they were **over charged**. This is recorded in the **sales returns journal**. When posting, the individual figure is credited to the debtor's account and it reduces what they owe. The debit entry is made as part of the **total** from sales returns journal, to sales returns account. It has the same effect as a credit note sent to a debtor in response to goods returned, or correcting an overcharge.

A Debit Note sent to Creditors

This is a debit note sent by a business to a creditor when returning goods, or when it discovers it was overcharged. The subsidiary book is the **purchases returns journal**. When posting, it's debited to the creditor's account and the debt reduces. The credit entry is made as part of the total from purchases returns journal, to purchases returns account.

A Debit Note received from Creditors

The business receives a debit note from a creditor to correct an **undercharge,** or for **not returning packaging containers** that were not part of the goods invoiced. It's treated like an **invoice received** and it's recorded in the purchases journal. It's posted to the credit side of the creditor's account and it increases the debt. The debit entry is made as part of the total from purchases journal, to purchases account.

Below is a summary about the use of a debit note;

	Debit Note to Debtors		Debit Note from Debtors
1.	Corrects sales undercharge	1.	Corrects sales overcharge
2.	For not returning packaging containers	2.	For sales returns
3.	Recorded in sales journal	3.	Recorded in sales returns journal

	Debit Note to Creditors		Debit Note from Creditors
1.	Corrects purchases overcharge	1.	Corrects purchases undercharge
2.	For purchases returns	2.	For not returning packaging containers to a Creditor
3.	Recorded in purchases returns journal	3.	Recorded in purchases journal

EXERCISE 8C. Write the following transactions in Subsidiary books
2nd Bought stock from Goodness for $280
3rd Sold goods to Patson for $210
5th Sent a debit note to Goodness for returns of $12
6th Purchased goods from Ali for $170
8th Made sales for $320 to Portia
9th Sent a credit note to Patson to correct an overcharge of $20

10th Sold goods to Rosetta for $270
14th Bought goods from Bernard for $390
15th Sent a credit note for $10 to Rosetta to correct an overcharge
16th Received an allowance from Ali for $25
17th Sold goods to Cedric for $295
19th Bernard sent a debit note for $40 to correct an undercharge
20th Sent a credit note to Portia for an allowance of $15
22nd Cedric returned goods for $30

8.8   Allowances

An allowance is a reduction in the amount supposed to be paid by a buyer. It's aimed at convincing the buyer **not to return** goods they are not satisfied with.

When a business gives an allowance, it writes and sends a **credit note** to a debtor. It's recorded in the sales returns journal. It's posted by crediting the debtor's account and this reduces what they owe. We write; **'Allowance'** in the details column to differentiate it from returns. The debit entry is made as part of the total to the sales returns account.

If the allowance is from a creditor then the business receives a credit note. It's recorded in the purchases returns journal. When posting, it's debited to the creditor's account and this reduces what is owed. We write; 'Allowance' in the details column. The credit entry is made as part of the total to purchases returns account.

8.9   Returns And The Trading Account

When some of the sales are returned by buyers /debtors then the sales figure reduces. So the total of sales returns are deducted from sales to get **net sales or turnover** as illustrated below;

Trading Account		
Sales		4,639
Sale Returns		- 73
Net Sales / Turnover		**4,566**
Opening Stock		405
Purchases	3,175	
Purchases Returns	- 47	
Net Purchases		+ 3,128
Goods available for Sale		3,533
Closing Stock		- 290
Cost of Sales		- 3,243
Gross Profit		**1,323**

Gross sales is the total on sales account before we deduct sales returns.

If some of purchases are returned to suppliers then the purchases figure has to reduce. So the total of purchases returns is deducted from purchases to get **net purchases** as illustrated above. Gross purchases is the total before deducting purchases returns.

According to the above trading account, we get gross profit by deducting cost of sales from net sales or turnover, and not from sales since we have sales returns.

To get goods available for sale, we add opening stock to net purchases, and **not** purchases since we have purchases returns.

Below is a summary of the source documents looked at so far, the subsidiary books, and their posting to the ledger;

Source Document	Subsidiary Book	Debit Entry	Credit Entry
Receipt written Cheque received Deposit slip	Cashbook	Cashbook	Income a/c /debtor a/c or asset sold
cheque stub Receipt recvd	Cashbook	Expense/creditor or asset bought	Cashbook
Invoice received Debit Note from creditor	Purchases Journal	Purchases a/c	Creditor a/c
Invoice sent Debit Note to debtor	Sales Journal	Debtor a/c	Sales a/c
Debit Note to creditor Credit Note recvd	Purchases Returns Journal	Creditor a/c	Purchases returns a/c
Credit Note sent Debit Note from debtor	Sales Returns Journal	Sales returns a/c	Debtor a/c

Multiple Choice and Short Answer Questions
1. A credit note from a supplier is recorded in
A   Sales returns journal.   B. Purchases account.
C. Purchases returns journal.   D. Returns inwards account
2. A debit note to a debtor is recorded by
A Crediting their account.   B. Debiting their account.
C. Debiting purchases account.   D. None of the above.
3. A total of the sales returns journal is posted to
A Credit side of the sales returns account
B Debit side of the sales returns account
C. Debit side of the purchases returns book
D. Debit side of the sales returns book
4. When a debtor returns goods we
A. Credit sales account and debit the debtors account
B. Credit sales returns account and credit the debtor

C. Credit the debtor and debit sales returns account
D. Credit the debtor and credit returns inwards boo.
5. Sales returns on the trading, profit and loss account is
A Deducted from sales   B. Added to purchases
C. Added to sales   D. Deducted from purchases
6. Which of the following is not recorded on the credit side of the trial balance?
A. Sales returns   B. Purchases returns
C. Rent received   D. Discount received.
7. Another term for sales returns is ………….........................…….
8. The document we send to a debtor who has returned goods is a
………….............
9. When we send a debit note to a customer it means the balance on their account will …………...
10. An error where an invoice of $150 is given instead of $130, is corrected by sending a …………...
11. The subsidiary book where credit notes received are recorded is a…………..................................
12. What are;   [a] returns   [b] allowances
13. Differentiate between the following;
[a] debit note and credit note. [b] undercharge and overcharge
14.   Explain the process of posting;
[a] the purchase returns journal   [b] the sales returns journal
15. What is the effect of purchases returns and of sales returns on the trading account?

EXERCISE 8D. Abigail started business with $230 cash, $320 stock, $4,250 bank and closing stock $440.
The following transactions took place during July 2001
2nd Paid $550 for rent by cheque
3rd Purchased stock for $275 by cheque
4th Bought goods from Natasha for $450
5th Sold goods to Peace for $590
6th Received a debit note from Natasha for $50 to correct an undercharge
8th Goods were sold to Alfred for $640
9th Sent debit note for $70 to Peace correcting an undercharge
10th Stock was bought from Teresa for $380
11th Paid Natasha by cheque for $300 less 10%
12th Received a debit note from Alfred with returns for $25
13th Received a cash commission of $86
15th Teresa sent a credit note for $20 correcting an overcharge
18th Peace paid $500 by cheque less 12%
20th Paid $37 cash for postages
21st Purchased stock from Felicia for $345
22nd Sold goods for a cheque of $350
23rd Made sales to Agnes for $430

24th Sent a debit note to Felicia with goods worth $35
25th Paid cash $78 for insurance premium
26th Sent a credit note to Agnes for an allowance of $15
27th A cheque for $278 was sent to Felicia in full settlement
28th Received a cheque for $400 less 8% from Alfred
30th Paid cash $38 for interest on delayed payments.
Required -write subsidiary books and post to the ledger
- balance accounts and extract a trial balance
- compile a trading profit and loss account.

Past Paper Question 1998

8. Enter the following in the personal accounts ONLY. Balance the personal accounts and write down the names of debtors and creditors.

Sept. 1   Sales on credit to D. Wamala 458, J. Moitse 235, G. Gama 98.
2nd   Purchases on credit A. Winter 77, H. Simelane 231,
P. Owuma 65.
8th   Sales on credit to J. Moitse 444, F. Fakudze 249
10th   Purchases on credit from H. Simelane 12, O. Olive 222.
12th   Returns inwards from G. Gama 9, J. Moitse 26.
17th   We returned goods to H. Simelane 24, O. Olive 12
20th   We paid A. Winter by cheque 77
24th   D. Wamala paid us by cheque   300.
26th   We paid O. Olive by cash   210
28th   D. Wamala paid us by cash 100.
30th   F. Fakudze pays us by cheque 249

Past Paper Question 1995

6A. The following balances were extracted from the books of Mr Nzuza. You are required to prepare a trial balance as at 31st December 1994.

Purchases	309	Sales	255
Returns inwards	16	Returns outwards	15
Motsa and Sons [cr]	141	Mr. Sangweni [dr]	29
Cash	57		

ANSWERS

8A
Purchases Returns Journal

6	Yvone	36	
11	Fortune	23	
17	Malcolm	40	
22	Cyprian	17	
	Cr Purchases Returns		116

8B
Sales Returns Journal

8	Sidney		29
14	Victor		42
19	Norah		38
25	Timothy		25
	Dr Sales Returns	134	

THE GENERAL JOURNAL

9.1   Introduction

The General Journal is a multipurpose subsidiary book where any kind of transaction is recorded before posting to the ledger. We have looked at subsidiary books with specialised uses as summarised below;

Subsidiary Book	Function
Cashbook	Cash transactions
Purchases Journal	Credit purchases
Sales Journal	Credit sales
Purchases Returns Journal	Purchases returned to Creditors
Sales Returns Journal	Sales returned by Debtors

All the other transactions which don't fit in any of the specialised subsidiary books are recorded in the general journal, and that's why we say it's multipurpose. It accommodates **all transactions that don't involve the exchange of cash,** with the exception of stock purchases, sales, and their returns.

It's used for recording opening statements, assets bought and sold on credit, correction of errors, adjustments, bad debts, interest charged, depreciation, stock drawings, and others.

9.2   Journal Entries And Narrations

Whatever we record in the general journal is in form of a journal entry.
A journal entry is a recording in the general journal where we indicate the account to be debited, the account to be credited, and a narration. This recording is based on **double entry** and follows the procedure below;
♦   the account to be debited is recorded on the first line with its amount in
         the debit column,
♦   the account to be credited on the second line with its amount in the credit
         column,
♦   next is the narration on the third line, and

◆ lastly we draw a line after the narration. This is to separate one journal entry from the next one.

Below is an illustration of a journal entry;

Date	Details	Dr	Cr
	Name of account to be **debited**	Amount	
	Name of account to be **credited**		Amount
	Narration		

A narration is a written explanation that helps to understand the kind of transaction which took place. Every transaction in the general journal should have a narration. This is necessary because it contains all sorts of transactions and nobody is always there to explain each one of them. Some of them are rare, while others are complicated. It's very helpful to the different users of accounts, let alone those who prepare them.

For example, a car is bought on credit from VW Motors at $4,000, we debit the Motor Vehicles account and credit the VW Motors account. The narration could be, "Car bought on credit", and lastly draw a line as illustrated below;

Date	Details	Dr	Cr
	Motor vehicles	4,000	
	VW Motors		4;000
	Car bought on credit		

If the business sold an unwanted machine to Apex Equipment Company on credit for $250, we record Apex Equipment Company first and its amount in the debit column. We then write Equipment with its amount in the credit column. Next is a narration and lastly a line as illustrated below;

Date	Details	Dr	Cr
	Apex Equipment Company	250	
	Equipment		250
	Equipment sold on credit		

The procedure of recording transactions in the general journal is also known as **journalising.**

9.3   Posting Journal Entries

Posting specialised journals saves time since the second entry is just the total. However, for the general journal **we post each and every amount individually**. The amount in the debit column is posted separately and the amount in the credit column is posted separately, to satisfy double entry. To avoid omitting any of the many transactions in the general journal, we **tick** each one that has been posted to the ledger.

According to the first journal entry above, the amount in the debit column is debited to the account written in the details column, and that is the Motor Vehicles account. In the details column of this account, we write the name of the account where the corresponding entry is recorded, and that is VW Motors.

The amount in the credit column is credited to the account whose name is in the details column and that is the VW Motors account. In the details column we write the name of the account where the corresponding entry is recorded, the Motor Vehicles. This applies to all journal entries and below is an illustration of the posting;

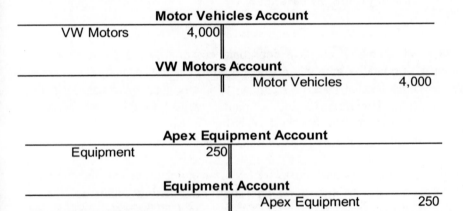

Motor Vehicles Account

| VW Motors | 4,000 | | |

VW Motors Account

| | | Motor Vehicles | 4,000 |

Apex Equipment Account

| Equipment | 250 | | |

Equipment Account

| | | Apex Equipment | 250 |

9.4   Opening Statements

Before a business can start keeping accounting records based on the double entry system, it has to start with **an opening statement**. This is a list of assets, liabilities and capital in a business just before it starts keeping double entry accounting records. Its prepared basing on the accounting equation of **A = C + L**. When the two totals of this equation are equal then it has balanced. If the opening statement doesn't balance then the trial balance and balance sheet will not balance.

A business can operate for some time without proper accounting records and this is common among the small one man businesses. Anytime they want double entry records they start with an opening statement.

It's only written at the beginning, in the general journal as illustrated below;

Date	Details	Dr	Cr
Jackson's Opening Statement as at 1st Jan. 2005			
	Machinery	1,320	
	Furniture	975	
	Stock	290	
	Debtors: Felicia	834	
	Martin	228	
	Thomson	637	
	Bank	1,769	
	Cash	86	
	Creditors: Keagan		507
	Victoria		496
	Rogers		369
	Capital		4,767
		6,139	6,139
	Being opening balances		

We start with items which have debit balances and they are; the fixed and current assets whose amounts are recorded in the debit column. The credit balance items are liabilities and capital, their amounts are recorded in the credit column. The name of the account is written in the details column besides the amount. We then find totals for the two sides which should be equal to balance. It's just like an **opening balance sheet**.

The general journal is the subsidiary book for opening statements. After we are satisfied that it balances, we post them as **opening balances** to their respective accounts in the Ledger. The amounts in the debit column are debited to accounts written in the details column. For example, $1,320 is debited to Machinery account while $975 is debited to Furniture account. The amounts in the credit column are credited to accounts written in the details column besides them. For example the $507 is credited to Keagan's account, while $4,767 is credited to the Capital account.

When posting an opening statement, all the asset amounts have their corresponding entries on the capital and liabilities accounts, and vice versa. However, you may not find any particular figure in the debit column corresponding to a particular figure in the credit column. It's only visible among the totals.

Opening statements are posted like any other entries in a subsidiary book. The only difference is that we write **"balance b/d"** in the details column as illustrated below;

Machinery Account		
Jan-01 Balance b/d	1,320	

Furniture Account		
Jan-01 Balance b/d	975	

Stock Account		
Jan-01 Balance b/d	290	

Felicia Account		
Jan-01 Balance b/d	834	

Martin Account		
Jan-01 Balance b/d	228	

Thomson Account		
Jan-01 Balance b/d	637	

Bank Account		
Jan-01 Balance b/d	1,769	

Cash Account		
Jan-01 Balance b/d	86	

keagan Account		
	Jan-01 Balance b/d	507

Victoria Account		
	Jan-01 Balance b/d	496

Rogers Account		
	Jan-01 Balance b/d	369

Capital Account		
	Jan-01 Balance b/d	4,767

Make sure every figure is posted otherwise the trial balance and balance sheet won't balance.

EXERCISE 9A. Using the following balances, write an opening statement and work out the capital. Post the opening statement to the ledger.
Cash   20   Bank   1,757

Furniture and Fittings	610	Creditors	979
Debtors	2,120	Stock	1,756
Plant and machinery	4,216	Loan	1,250

9.5   Non-Stock Credit Transactions

Stock bought on credit is recorded in the purchases journal, while credit sales are recorded in the sales journal. Stock returns are recorded in returns journals. All the other credit transactions involving **non-stock items** are recorded in the general journal as their subsidiary book.

This includes;

♦ **Assets bought or sold on credit.** For example, a Computer bought on credit from IQ Equipment for $430;

♦ **Expenses incurred on credit.** Examples are; stationery bought on credit from Top Shop for $75; advertising services for $120 provided by the General Times Newspapers and payment is later;

The above are journalised as illustrated below;

Furniture & fittings		430	
IQ Equipment			430
Computer bought on credit			
Stationery		75	
Top Shop			75
Stationery bought on credit			
Advertising		120	
General Times			120
Advertising service on credit			

EXERCISE 9B. You are **required** to write journal entries for the following transactions. Narrations are not required.

3rd Bought a house from National housing Corporation on credit for $32,000

6th Purchased stationery for $53 from Santos Bookshop on credit

8th Bought furniture from Lewis Furnitures for $1,300 on credit

12th Purchased machines from Konica for $635

17th Sold extra furniture to Willis for $250

9.6   Error Correction

An error is a posting or calculation that was not done correctly. The general journal is the subsidiary book used for **correction of errors** in the ledger.

Some errors are exposed by trial balance totals. An investigation is carried out to identify all the errors.

After the errors are discovered, they are not corrected by crossing out or using correction fluid. They are **corrected starting with a journal entry** in the general journal, before posting to the ledger. However, this is beyond the coverage of this book.

9.7   Stock Drawings And Donations

The subsidiary book for cash taken for personal use is the cashbook. The subsidiary book for stock taken for personal use is the general journal. Below is an illustration of the journal entry;

Drawings	85	
Purchases		85
Goods taken for personal use		

When posting we debit the drawings account and credit the purchases account. When we balance the purchases account, the amount transferred to the trading account is reduced. We don't credit the sales account because they were **not sold**.

Donations are goods given out free. It's not a sale and we don't credit the sales account. This transaction is recorded in the general journal and below is an illustration of the journal entry;

Donations	320	
Purchases		320
Stock given away as a donation		

We debit donations account and credit purchases account. This is an expense to the business and it's recorded on the profit and loss account.

9.8   Interest Charged

The business charges interest to debtors for **delayed payments,** and creditors also charge the business for the same. The subsidiary book for these transactions is the general journal.

Debtors: A debtor is charged interest for failure to pay their debt within the agreed period of time. This is done by sending them an invoice for the amount of interest with an explanation like; **"interest on overdue debt"**. This interest increases what the debtor owes. For example, the interest charged is 4% on an outstanding debt of $1,450, which comes to $58. The journal entry for this is illustrated below;

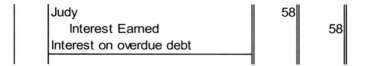

Judy	58	
Interest Earned		58
Interest on overdue debt		

The debtor is debited with $58 while the interest earned account is credited as illustrated below;

Judy Account

| Sales | 1,450 | |
| Interest earned | 58 | |

Interest Earned Account

| | Judy | 58 |

Creditors: If the business takes long to pay then a creditor charges interest and this increases the debt. So the business receives an invoice from the creditor reading; "interest on overdue debt". Let's assume the interest charged is 2.5% on a debt of $1,268 which comes to $31.70.

In the journal entry and the ledger, the interest paid account is debited while the creditor account is credited as illustrated below;

Interest paid	31.70	
Richard		31.70
Interest on overdue account		

In addition to purchases of $1,268, the journal entry is posted to the ledger account as illustrated below;

Interest Paid

| Richard | 31.70 | |

Richard Account

| | Purchases | 1,268.00 |
| | Interest paid | 31.70 |

9.9   Adjustments

The General Journal is also used as a subsidiary book for adjustments made before preparing the final accounts. **Adjustments** are additions or subtractions made to ledger account balances in order to get the correct figures for the final accounts. These are explained in chapter 13.

The different functions of the General Journal
1 Opening Statements
2 Non-Stock Credit Transactions
3 Error Correction
4 Stock Drawings and Donations
5 Interest Charged
6 Adjustments

Multiple Choice and Short Answer Questions

1. Which of the following is not part of a journal entry?

A.   the account to be debited   B. the posting

C.   the account to be credited   D. the narration

2. The subsidiary book for stock sold on credit is

A   sales journal   B. cashbook

C. general journal   D. purchases journal

3. All these are found in an opening statement except

A. expenses   B. assets   C. liabilities   D. capital

4. When a debtor is charged interest the amount they owe...................

A. decreases   B. doesn't change

C. disappears   D. increases

5. The subsidiary book for assets bought on credit is

A. sales journal   B. purchases journal

C. general journal   D. cashbook

6. For each of the following transactions, indicate which subsidiary book they should go to.

a) Sale of goods for $650.

b) Sale of a company car on credit for $7,500.

c) Payment of $500 wages by cheque.

d) Settlement of a supplier's debt with cash of $750.

e) Withdrawal of stock worth $140 for personal use.

f) Purchase of goods for $1,200 from suppliers on credit.

7. Match the journal entry with the appropriate narration below;

Journal Entries.

		Dr	Cr
(a)	Drawings	850	
	Purchases		850
(b)	Motor vehicles	1200	
	Nissan Motors		1200
(c)	Creditors	395	
	Bank		395
(d)	Bank	475	
	Discount allowed	25	
	Debtors		500
(e)	Purchases	1100	
	Creditors		1100
(f)	Returns inwards	500	
	Debtors		500
(g)	Purchases	65	
	Cash		65

Narrations

i) Paid a supplier's debt by cheque.

ii) Goods taken for private use.

iii) Stock bought for cash

iv) Debtor pays less $25 discount.

v) Car bought on credit.

vi) Goods bought on credit.

vii) Sales returned.

8. Explain each of the following; [a] general journal   [b] journal entry

[c] journalising   [d] narration   [e] opening statement

9. What are the differences between interest earned and interest paid?

10. Draw a chart to show the different types of subsidiary books. Give an explanation for each of them.

EXERCISE 9C. Journalise the following transactions for the month ended April 2006 including narrations.

5th Purchased a motor bike from Carson wheels for $12,000

8th Sent an invoice of $23 to Stella for delayed payments

12th Bought stationery from Green Bookshop for $47

16th Xerox supplied a typewriter for $1,250.

20th Donated stock valued at $420

23rd Earned a commission of $270 for stock sold on behalf of Big Bend Suppliers.

26th Received an invoice of $18 from Carry for delayed payment

29th Sold used furniture to Tamara for $380

PPQ 2005

2. Mzimela started a business on October 2002 with the following:
Buildings E3040, Furniture E3240, Bank overdraft E2200, Creditors
were Phumaphi E1480, Mphikwa E2465 and Vumani E2755.

Oct 2nd	Bought goods from Phumaphi	E712
4th	Bought stock from Mphikwa E900	
5th	Sent a debit note to Phumaphi with returns for E68	
7th	Bought stock from Vumani E1125	
8th	Sent a debit note to Vumani to correct an overcharge of E45	
8th	Received a credit note for an allowance of E90 from	

Mphikwa
Required: Prepare an opening statement to
(i) calculate Mzimela's capital   (7)
(ii) write out all subsidiary books. (8)
(No ledger accounts required)

PPQ 2004

1. Journalize the following transaction. Dates and narrations must
be included.
Jan 4 Write off as bad debts 300-00 from debtors.
Jan 4 The business purchased typewriter from E. Chrambains 4000-00.
Jan 7 XYZ charged interest on goods purchased 100-00.
Jan 10 Motor Van is to be depreciated by 3000-00 of the cost price of
12000-00.
Jan 20 Fittings 4000-00 is to be depreciated by 5%.   [15]

PPQ 2002

6b Prepare an opening statement from the following information.
Also determine the capital figure.   [7]

Purchases	200
Wages	300
Debtors	400
Creditors	250
Bank overdraft	50
Sales	200

PPQ 2001

8. Show by means of journal entries how you would record the
following:
Mar 4 Received an invoice of R720 from Woodlands for office table.
Mar 6 Stationery bought on credit for R475 has been wrongly
entered in the purchases book.

Mar 8   A transaction on purchases of R750 from T.A. Suppliers has been wrongly recorded as R570.

Mar 9   Received a bill from Compu-tech. Repairs for servicing an office Computer R186

Mar 10   Londa cannot be traced to clear his debt. Write off his account of R230.

PPQ 2000

4.   The assets and liabilities of Mangwe Bricks, owned by Joe Mangwe on 1 September 2000 are shown below.

Cash held R20; Cash at bank R1,300; Stock R3,750; Bhembe owed the business R46; while Mamba owed R167. On the other hand, the business had the following bills to settle: Masuku R405 and Shezi R68.

You are **required to:**

i) Prepare an opening statement of Mangwe Bricks.

ii) Open ledger accounts in the business' books.

PPQ 1997

4.   Show by means of journal entries how you would record the following:

Oct,4.   The correction for 200 repairs to motor van posted to the debit of motor vehicles account.

6. The purchase of a motor van on credit from Tracar Ltd for 30,000.

8. Discount shown as 60 on the credit side of the cashbook , posted to the credit of the discount allowed account.

10. Sale of second hand van to Tracar Ltd for 3,000.

15. Discount deducted on payment of Maziya's account, 20 has been disallowed by him.

18.   2,500 has been included in wages account and 5,000 in purchases account in respect of an extension to the office premises.

PPQ 1996

6a. The following entries have been made in the Journal of Mr Sangweni;

March 30 Bad debts account	200	
T. Ruka		200
Mar 28 Drawings account	75	
Stock account		75
Mar 29 T.M. Co [Ltd]	1700	
Machinery		1700
Mar 30 Depreciation	250	
Furniture & fixtures		250
Mar 31 Trading account	2500	

Stock   *2500*
Give an explanation of each entry in the form of a brief narration.

ANSWERS

9A The Opening Statement

Cash	20	
Bank	1,757	
Debtors	2,120	
Stock	1,756	
Plant & Machinery	4,216	
Furniture & fittings	610	
Creditors		979
Loan		1,250
Capital		**8,250**
	10,479	10,479
Being opening balances		

THE LEDGER

Debtors Account

1	Balance b/d	2,120		

Stock Account

1	Balance b/d	1,756		

Plant & Machinery Account

1	Balance b/d	4,216		

Furniture & Fittings Account

1	Balance b/d	610		

Creditors Account

			1	Balance b/d	979

Loan Account

			1	Balance b/d	1,250

Capital Account

			1	Balance b/d	8,250

The Cashbook

Date	Receipts	DA	Cash	Bank	Date	Payments	DR	Cash	Bank
1	Balances b/d		20	1,757					

9B

3	Buildings	32,000	
	National Housing Corp		32,000
6	Stationery	53	
	Sebec Bookshop		53
8	Furniture & Fittings	1,300	
	Lewis Furnitures		1,300
12	Machinery	635	
	Konica		635
17	Willis	250	
	Furniture & Fittings		250

CHAPTER 10

THE THREE COLUMN CASHBOOK

This chapter covers: **page**

10.1   Introduction

The cashbook in chapter 3 is a **two column cashbook** where one column is for cash transactions and the other is for bank transactions. To become a **three column cashbook** it must have an extra column on the debit side for recording discount allowed, and an extra column on the credit side for recording discount received as illustrated below;

Dr										Cr
Date	Receipts	Fo	Discount Allowed	Cash	Bank	Date	Payments	Fo	Discount Received	Cash	Bank

Discount is a reduction in the amount charged. We have a trade discount, quantity discount, and cash discount.

Trade Discount is a reduction in price charged for goods bought in large quantities for **trade** or re-sale. It's only allowed to traders. In accounts we only record the net amount, which is after deducting the discount. We don't record the trade discount. If an invoice has a trade discount, the gross total before the discount is not considered.

A Quantity Discount is a reduction in the price charged for goods bought in large quantities. It's allowed to any buyer taking in large quantities. It's also not recorded in accounts.

A Cash Discount is a reduction in the amount if payment is made within a specified period of time. It's aimed at encouraging quick payments. It's expressed as a percentage of the amount due and it's only allowed if payment is on time. It's also known as a **settlement discount**.

The discount recorded in the cashbook is the cash discount. This is because it's allowed or received against the amounts recorded in the cash or bank column.

10.2   Discount Allowed And Received

Discount Allowed is a reduction in the amount paid by debtors, as a reward for prompt payment. It's allowed to debtors. If payment is not within the specified period then the discount is not allowed. It's treated as an **expense** since it reduces the income to be received by the business. It's what the business gives away, to encourage debtors pay promptly. It's like the debtor pays the full amount and then the business pays back the amount of the discount. **The source document** is the receipt copy, where the cash and discount allowed are recorded.

Discount Received is a reduction in the amount paid to creditors, as a reward for prompt payment. It's received by the business and it's treated as an **income**. It's like the business pays the whole amount and then the creditor pays back the discount. The source document is the **receipt received** where the cash paid, and the discounts are recorded.

10.3   Discount Calculations

Discounts are normally expressed as a **percentage** of the amount owed. In the word percent, **per** means **"for every"**, and **cent** is short form for **century** which is **100(years)**. Therefore, **percent** implies **"for every 100"**. Instead of the word **percent** we often use it's symbol **" %"**.

If a discount is 5%, it implies the amount to be paid is reduced by $5 for every $100. So out of every $100, only $95 is paid, the $5 is a discount.
To get the money discount we have to calculate and we can follow the procedure below;
♦ Establish the initial amount to be paid as being equal to **100%**;
♦ **Divide** both the 100% and the amount by **100** in order to get the value equivalent to 1% (in short divide the amount by 100);
♦ **Multiply** both the 1% and its equivalent, by the **stated percentage** to get the discount amount (multiply the equivalent by the percentage).

To get **5% of $1500** using the above procedure;
100% = 1,500

100% ÷100 = 1%	1,500 ÷100 = 15.00	therefore; **1% = 15**
1% x 5 = 5%	15 x 5 = 75	therefore; **5% = 75**

And so; **5% of $1,500 is $75.** The amount paid is **1,425 = 1,500 -75**.

A more straight formula is by making the discount percentage the **numerator** and the 100% the **denominator**-- don't include the % symbol. We then multiply this **fraction** by the total amount to be paid.

For example, 2.5% of $300 can be calculated as follows;

$2.5 \div 100 \times 300 = \$7.50$

The simplest way is by use of a calculator. Enter the amount, press the multiplication sign, enter the discount, and press the % sign. The answer is displayed immediately.

Payment in full settlement is a situation where the amount paid is less than the debt but the whole debt is settled in full. So the **difference** between the debt and the amount paid is a **discount**.

If a debtor owes $450 and pays $400 in full settlement, the difference between the two is $50 and that is the **discount allowed**.

If a business owes $1,200 and pays only $1,100 in full settlement, the difference of $100 is a **discount received**.

10.4   Discounts And The Cashbook

Discount allowed is recorded on the debit side, while discount received is recorded on the credit side of the cashbook. A discount is allowed or received together with a particular payment. So Discount allowed is written in its column but on the same line as the amount received.

Discount received is written in its column but on the same line as the amount paid. When we add the discount and the amount paid in the cash or bank column, the total we get is the debt they cleared. The totals for the discount allowed and discount received are written on the line just below the totals for the cash and bank columns as illustrated below;

Dr											Cr
Date	Receipts	Fo	Discount Allowed	Cash	Bank	Date	Payments	Fo	Discount Received	Cash	Bank
3	Nadia		3.00		117.00	6	Stewart		1.50	73.50	
9	Kate		15.00		295.00	12	Linda		12.50		237.50
14	Timothy		1.50	98.50		17	Newton		10.00		100.00
							Balances	c/d		25.00	74.50
				98.50	412.00					98.50	412.00
	Dr disc.allowed a/c		19.50				Cr disc. received a/c		24.00		

Please note that discount columns are not balanced, we just find their totals. The entries in the cashbook above are based on the following transactions. The debtors owe as follows; Nadia $175, Kate $310, and Timothy $100. The creditor's owed are; Stewart $250, Linda $320 and Newton $110.

Oct 3rd Nadia paid $120 by cheque less 2.5% discount
Oct 6th Paid 75 cash to Stewart less 2% discount
Oct 9th Kate paid $295 by cheque in full settlement.
Oct 12th Paid 250 by cheque to Linda less 5% discount
Oct 14th Timothy paid 100 by cash less 1.5% discount.
Oct 17th Paid 100 by cheque to Newton in full settlement

The calculations are;
3rd 2.5% of $120 = $3
6th 2% of $75 = $1.5
9th $295 clears a debt of $310   :- the discount is   310 -295 = $15
12th 5% of $250 = $12.5
14th 1.5% of $100 = $1.5
17th $100 clears a debt of $110   :- the discount is 110 -100 = $10

EXERCISE 10A
Record the following transactions in Dan's cashbook for the month of April 2006 and balance it.
4th Received a cheque from Gordon for 1,200 less 10% discount
6th Sent a cheque to Mark for 840 less 5% discount
7th Mason cleared his debt of 1,800 by cheque less 20% discount
9th Paid Allan 1,500 less 15% discount by cheque
14th Received a cheque from Mason for a debt of 800 less 12.5% discount
17th Sent a cheque to Lydia for 600 less 17% discount
20th Daniel paid cash 500 less 9% discount
26th Paid Mathew 400 cash less 3% discount

10.5   Posting Discount Allowed

Although the cashbook is part of the ledger, the **discount columns** in the cashbook are **not part of the ledger**. We use the cashbook as a subsidiary book, to enable the **addition** of the many discounts before their total is posted. So the entry in the discount columns is **not part of double entry**.

The discount allowed and the payments received from a debtor are part of the same transaction. They are recorded on the same source document, and both recorded on the debit side of the cashbook. So they are both credited to the debtor's account who is the giver. The discount allowed is recorded just below the debtor's payment and when you add the two you get the total debt they cleared. This makes the **first entry for the discount allowed** in the ledger, and below is an illustration of its posting from the cashbook in section 10.4;

Nadia Account

1-Oct	Balance b/d	175.00	3	Bank	117.00
			3	Discount Allowed	3.00
			31	Balance c/d	55.00
		175.00			175.00
1-Nov	Balance b/d	55.00			

Kate Account

1-Oct	Balance b/d	310.00	9	Bank	295.00
			9	Discount Allowed	15.00
		310.00			310.00

Timothy Account

1-Oct	Balance b/d	100.00	14	Cash	98.50
			14	Discount Allowed	1.50
		100.00			100.00

Please note that the accounts show the discount allowed, the amount paid, the amount owed previously, and the closing balance.

The second entry for all the discounts allowed for that month is their total that is posted from the debit side of the cashbook, to the **debit side** of the discount allowed account. Take note of the instruction in the cashbook receipts column to; **'Debit Discount Allowed Account'**. This posting is done after calculating the month's total and it's illustrated below;

Discount Allowed Account

31-Oct	Debtors	19.50

10.6   Posting Discount Received

The discount received and payment to a creditor is part of the same transaction. They are recorded on the same source document and both recorded on the credit side of the cashbook. They are both debited to the creditor's account who is the receiver. The discount is recorded just below the payment, and when you add the two you get the total debt cleared. This makes the **first entry for discount received** in the ledger, and below is an illustration of its posting from the cashbook in section 10.4

Stewart Account

6	Cash	73.50	1-Oct	Balance b/d	250.00
6	Discount	1.50			
31	Balance c/d	175.00			
		250.00			250.00
			1-Nov	Balance b/d	175.00

Linda Account

12	Bank	237.50	1-Oct	Balance b/d	320.00
12	Discount	12.50			
31	Balance c/d	70.00			
		320.00			320.00
			1-Nov	Balance b/d	70.00

Newton Account

17	Bank	100.00	1-Oct	Balance b/d	110.00
17	Discount	10.00			
		110.00			110.00

Please note; the accounts show the discount received, the amount paid, the amount owed previously, and the closing balance.

The second entry for all discounts received that month is their total. It's posted from the credit side of the cashbook, to the **credit side** of the discount received account. Take note of the instruction in the cashbook payments column to; **'Credit Discount Received Account'**. This posting is done after calculating the month's total and it's illustrated below;

Discount Received Account

	31-Oct Creditors	24.00

EXERCISE 10B
On 1st July 2002, James started business with $11,780 at the bank and cash of $350. During the month he recorded the following transactions;
July   8th Jones a debtor paid his debt of 320 by cheque less 5% discount.
10th   Bought a van for 2,500 paying by cheque.
12th   Paid wages of 50 in cash.
13th   Made cash sales 35.
15th   Received a cheque of 200 from Daniel in full settlement of 220.
18th   Paid Raymond's account of 155 less 15 discount by cash.
19th   Received a cheque of 500 from Elvis less 25 discount.

19th   Made cash sales for 20.
19th   Paid wages of 75 cash.
20th   Paid Marina's account 600 by cheque less 20% discount.
22nd   Cash purchases 85.
25th   Paid Martin's account of 350 by cheque less 2% discount.
27th   Received cash payment of 275 from Elvis.
28th   Bought goods worth 500 by cheque receiving 15% cash
       discount.
28th   Paid cash 60 for stationery.
31st   Paid wages by cheque 3,000.
31st   Paid rent with cash 100.
31st   Drew a cheque of 500 for personal expenses.
Required: Write up James' cashbook for July 2002.

10.7   Discounts And Final Accounts

Discount allowed account has a debit balance which is recorded among the
debit balances on the trial balance. It's what the business pays to encourage
prompt payment and it's an **expense**. It's recorded on the **profit and loss**
account and added to the other business expenses.

Discount received account has a credit balance which is recorded among the
credit balances on the trial balance. It's a reward for prompt payment and it's
an **income** to the business. It's recorded on the **profit and loss** account and
added as another income to get total income. The two discounts are illustrated
below;

Trading, Profit & Loss Account		
Sales		742.00
Opening stock	125.00	
Purchases	400.00	
Goods available for sale	525.00	
Closing stock	204.00	
Cost of sales		321.00
Gross Profit		421.00
Commission Earned		155.00
Discount Received		**24.00**
Total Income		600.00
Operating Expenses		
Stationery	68.00	
Telephone	115.00	
Discount Allowed	**19.50**	
Sundry expenses	45.50	
Total Expenses		248.00
Net Profit		352.00

10.8   Dishonoured Cheques

A **Dishonoured Cheque** is one against which the bank **refuses** to make payment. There are several reasons for this and they include; insufficient funds, conflicting amounts, wrong signature, instructions not to pay, unconfirmed alterations, and others.

When a cheque is received it's taken to the bank. The amount is debited to the cashbook and credited to the debtors account. However, if a cheque is dishonoured the bank sends it to the depositor stamped with **"R/D".** This is an abbreviation for **"Refer to Drawer"** and it instructs the depositor to solve the problem with the one who paid.

A dishonoured cheque is accompanied by an **"advice of unpaid cheque."** It contains detailed information about the cheque and it's the source document. Below is an illustration;

NATIONAL BANK LTD	ADVICE OF UNPAID CHEQUE
	Branch................................
Debit/ Depositor..............................	Date..................................
....	Date of deposit.....................
Account No...............................	Amount............................
Cheque Serial No..........................	Drawn by...........................
With answer.................................	
Drawers Bank............................	Branch.............................
Check Clerk..................................	Clerk Initials........................
Accountant..................................	

This dishonoured cheque is credited to the cashbook and we write the debtor's name followed by **R/D** in the details column as illustrated below;

Date	Receipts	Fo	Disc. Allow.	Cash	Bank	Date	Payments	Fo	Disc. Rcvd	Cash	Bank
10-Mar	Stella				340	20-Mar	Stella R/D				340

The bank balance had increased by $340 on the 10th. Crediting the dishonoured cheque on the 20th reduces back the balance.

The dishonoured cheque is posted by debiting the debtor's account as illustrated below;

Stella Account

1-Mar	Balance b/d	340	10-Mar	Bank	340
20-Mar	Bank R/D	340			

We write "Bank R/D" in the details column. The debt which had been cleared with a cheque on the 10th is re-instated by the dishonoured cheque on the 20th of March.

10.9   Bank Charges

Bank charges is money charged to customers for **services** provided by a bank. They include; maintaining accounts, paying standing orders, credit transfers, loans and over drafts, and others. For each of these services the bank has a different type of **charge** and examples are; a ledger fee, a service fee, a commission, administration fee, and others. These charges are recorded on a **bank statement** (chapter 14), which is sent to account holders every month end.

These charges are deducted from the account by the bank, and are an expense to the business. They are extracted from the bank statement which is the source document. They are recorded by crediting the cashbook, which is the subsidiary book. The debit entry is made to the Bank charges account. Below is an illustration;

Bank Charges Account

Bank	45

10.10   Bank Loan

A Loan is money borrowed from a bank or financial institution and repayment is normally between six months and five years or more. Some banks require security before they give out loans. **Security** is property which the bank can sell to recover its money in case the borrower fails to pay back the whole amount. Examples of security are land and buildings. The subsidiary book for a bank loan is the cashbook which is debited. The credit entry is made on the loan account and it's a **long-term liability**.

The bank charges interest and the loan is repaid in equal monthly instalments. The monthly repayment is made up of part of the loan and interest, and both are credited to the cashbook. The loan repaid is debited to the Loan account until it's all repaid and the account closed. The interest paid is debited to the Interest on Loan account. The balances on both accounts are recorded on the trial balance. The interest is an expense to the business and it's recorded on the profit and loss account. The balance on the loan account is recorded on the balance sheet among the liabilities.

Below is an illustration of the loan account with 3 monthly instalments;

Loan Account

30/Apr	Bank	1,250	1/Apr	Bank	30,000
	Balance c/d	28,750			
		30,000			30,000
31/May	Bank	1,250		Balance b/d	28,750
	Balance c/d	27,500			
		28,750			28,750
30/Jun	Bank	1,250		Balance b/d	27,500
	Balance c/d	26,250			
		27,500			27,500
				Balance c/d	26,250

$30,000 is the original amount borrowed. The $1,250 is the monthly instalment towards the repayment of the loan excluding interest. The loan balance after 3 instalments is $26,250.

10.11   The Cashbook's Importance

1. The cashbook is the subsidiary book for all cash and cheque transactions. They are all recorded there before posting to the ledger.

2.   Its the most important book since that is where we record the most important/ sensitive asset of the business, **money**. No business can survive without money.

3. It shows when a bank overdraft was acquired and when it was paid back.

4. Its the subsidiary book for discount received and discount allowed.

5. Its the subsidiary book for bank charges.

6. Its the subsidiary book for loans received and paid back.

Multiple Choice and Short Answer Questions

1. Discount received is recorded
A. As expense on profit and loss account   B. On balance sheet
C. As income on profit and loss account   D. None of these
2.   30 items are sold at a price of $15 each with a 10% trade discount. If 4 items are returned, what amount is still owed?
A. $351   B. $450   C. $405   D. $375.
3. A discount allowed is given to
A. creditors   B. suppliers   C. banks   D. debtors
4. Bank charges can be any of the following except
A. ledger fees   B. service fee
C. opening an account   D. commission

5. Which of the following is **not one** of the three columns in a cashbook?
A. the cash column   B. the receipts column
C. the discount column   D. the bank column

6. If we received a cheque of 2,500 less 5% discount from Melca. All the following are correct except?
A. Melca paid 2,500   B. Melca paid 2,375
C. Melca owed 2,500   D. Melca received a discount of 125.

7. If the list price of goods is $5,000, the trade discount is 10% and the cash discount is 2%. what is the lowest amount payable for the goods?
A. 3,960   B. 4,500   C. 4,400   D. 4,410.

8. The double entry for a discount received is;

Debit	Credit
A. Discount Received	Creditors
B. Debtors	Discount Received
C. Creditors	Discount Received
D. Discount Received	Debtors

9. Discount.........................appears on the credit side of the cashbook, while discount...........................is shown on the receipts side.

10. The total of the .... is debited to the discount allowed account in the ledger.

11. Individual amounts in the discount column on the payments side of the cashbook are credited to... accounts.

12. Explain the following;
[a] a discount   [b] payment in full settlement   [c] bank charges

13. Differentiate between the following;
[a] three column cashbook and a two column cashbook
[b] trade discount and cash discount
[c] discount allowed account and discount allowed column

14. What is the procedure of posting discount received to the ledger?

15. What is a dishonoured cheque?

EXERCISE 10C Millicent started business on the 1st of May 2003 with cash 780, bank balance of 6,300 and stock valued at 241. Her closing stock was 160. From the following transactions, you are required to;
[i] write her subsidiary books   [ii] post to the ledger
[iii] extract a trial balance   [iv] compile a trading, profit and loss account.

2nd   Paid rent 800 by cheque
3rd   Bought stock for re-sale using cash 360
4th   Sold goods for cash 155
5th   Purchased stock from Harold for 515
6th   Sold goods to Tobias for 460
8th   Stock for 380 was sold to Lulu
9th   Sent a cheque to Harold for 485 in full settlement
10th   Received a cheque from Tobias for 460 less 15% discount
12th   Bought goods from Wilfred for 340

15th Stock was bought for 764 from Sebastian
16th Made sales to Patrick for 640
17th Goods were sold to Terrence for 520
19th Paid water bill 32 by cash
20th More stock was sold to Tobias for 485
21st A cheque was sent to Wilfred for 340 less 5%
22nd Paid cash 53 for stationery
23rd Received a cheque from Patrick for 500 less 3%
24th Bought more goods from Harold for 443
25th Sold stock for a cheque of 470
26th Paid 450 for wages by cheque
27th More goods were sold to Patrick for 860
28th Paid cash 43 for interest on delayed payment
29th Terrence paid 520 by cheque less 10% discount

PPQ 1993

4. Enter the following transactions in a three column cashbook

Jan. 1.	Cash at bank from previous month	271.00	
1	cash in hand from previous month	25.00	
1	Drew cheque for petty cash payments	10.00	
2	Bought office furniture for cheque	20.66	
	Received cheque from T Zwane		87.75
	Discount allowed him	2.25	
10	Paid cheque to Mr. S. Mmema	68.25	
10	Discount received from him	1.75	
15	Paid cash for wages	17.98	
18	Received cheque from F. Tsela	28.80	
18	Discount allowed	1.50	
19	Paid rent by cheque	15.44	
28	Drew from bank for office cash		10.00
31	Sold goods and received cheque`	110.19	
31	Paid into bank from office cash		5.00
31	Refunded petty cash by cheque		9.12
31	Drew cash from bank, 100 and paid it to staff as salaries.		[15]

PPQ 1997

5A. The cash account of Mr. Mazibuko for November, 1994 had been written up as shown below. Rewrite the account as it should be.

4	Received from S. Zulu	750	2	cash balance 1st Nov	360
6	Sundry expenses	175	5	cash sales	2,500
7	Paid N. Ngema	400	6	rent received	150
8	Deposited in bank	250	9	wages [paid]	350
19	Paid for advertising	200	11	cash sales	790
	balance c/d	2,410	20	received from B, Cele	75
		4,185			4,185
				balance b/d	2,410

10A Dan's Cashbook for the month of April 2006

Date	Receipts	DA	Cash	Bank	Date	Payments	DR	Cash	Bank
4	Gordon	120		1,080	6	Mark	42		798
7	Mason	360		1,440	9	Allan	225		1,275
14	Mason	100		700	17	Lydia	102		498
20	Daniel	45	455		26	Mathew	12	388	
						Balances c/d		67	649
			455	3,220				455	3,220
	Dr DA A/c	625				Cr DR A/c	381		
	Balances b/d		67	649					

10B James' Cashbook for the month of July 2002

Date	Details	DA	Cash	Bank	Date	Details	DR	Cash	Bank
Jul-01	Bal b/d		350	11,780	Jul-10	Van			2,500
8	Jones	16		304	12	Wages		50	
13	Sales		35		18	Raymond	15	140	
15	Daniel	20		200	19	Wages		75	
19	Elvis	25		500	20	Marina	120		480
19	Sales		20		22	Purchases		85	
27	Elvis		275		25	Martin	7		343
					28	Purchases	75		425
					28	Stationery		60	
					31	Wages			3,000
					31	Rent		100	
					31	Drawings			500
						Balances c/d		170	5,536
			680	12,784				680	12,784
	Dr DA A/c	61				Cr DR A/c	217		
	Bals b/d		170	5,536					

CHAPTER 11

LEDGER CLASSIFICATION

11.1   Introduction

The Ledger is the main book of Accounts since that's where all transactions are posted. Because there are so many transactions and accounts, it was divided up and each section assigned to a particular Bookkeeper. So the recording of transactions could be shared among several Bookkeepers and the work completed in a shorter period of time. The ledger sections are illustrated below;

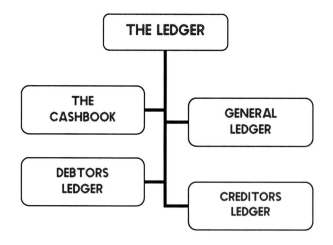

In a real business situation, each of these sections has its own ledger book. However, in a practice situation we have all the sections written in one ledger book except the cashbook. We, therefore, plan our work in such a way that when we start with the creditor's ledger, all its accounts follow each other before we start on the debtor's ledger. All the accounts in the debtor's ledger follow each other before we start the general ledger. Accounts belonging to different sections of the ledger should not be mixed up. Each of the sections should have a properly underlined heading.

The cashbook, as a section of the ledger, is covered extensively in chapters 3 and 10.

11.2   The Debtors And Creditors Ledger

The debtor's ledger is a section where we record accounts for **debtors only**. Most sales by large businesses are on credit and are recorded in this section. That is why it's referred to as the **sales ledger**. Everything to do with credit sales is recorded on individual debtors' accounts. There is more on the debtor's ledger in chapter 7 and 8.

The creditor's ledger is a section where we record accounts for **creditors only**. Most purchases by large businesses are on credit and they are recorded in this section. That is why it's referred to as the **purchases ledger**. Everything to do with credit purchases is recorded on individual creditors' accounts. There is more about the creditor's ledger in chapter 7 and 8.

11.3   The General Ledger

The General Ledger is a section where we record accounts for capital, drawings, income, expenses, fixed assets, stock, long term liabilities, and any other accounts. Therefore, any accounts which are not debtors, creditors, cash and bank, are recorded here. This section of the ledger is commonly known as the **Nominal Ledger.**

11.4   Types Of Accounts

We have several types of accounts and they are classified according to what is recorded on them. The major classifications are whether they are personal or impersonal accounts. Below is an illustration of their classifications;

TYPES OF ACCOUNTS

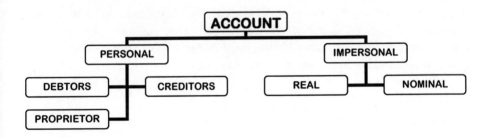

Personal Accounts

These are accounts where we record transactions involving individual people, other businesses, or institutions that buy or sell to the business. This includes debtor's accounts, creditor's accounts, and the proprietor's accounts. They are called personal accounts because there are people behind them.

Debtor's Accounts is where we record credit sales, sales returns, debtor payments, discounts, bad debts, and others.

Creditor's Accounts is where we record credit purchases, purchases returns, payments to creditors, discounts, undercharge, and others.

Proprietor Accounts is where we record the proprietor's (owner) investment into the business, and what they get out of it. What they invest is recorded on the **capital account**. What they get from the business is recorded on the **drawings account**.

Impersonal Accounts

This is a class of accounts where we record **assets, incomes and the expenses** of a business. They are classified into real accounts and nominal accounts.

Real Accounts

These are accounts where we record the **assets or properties** belonging to a business. They are said to be real because they are tangible items that can be **seen and touched**. This includes land and buildings, furniture and fittings, equipment, motor vehicles, bank, cash, stock, and others. These accounts are found in the general ledger, with the exception of the cash and bank accounts in the cashbook.

Nominal Accounts

These are accounts where we record the business **incomes** and **expenses**. Business incomes include; sales, rent received, commission earned, and others. Business expenses include; purchases, wages and salaries, rent paid, insurance, and others.

11.5   The Debit And Crediting Summary In The Ledger

ACCOUNT	WHEN IS IT DEBITED	WHEN IS IT CREDITED
Fixed assets	when bought	when sold
Cash	on receipt of cash	on payment of cash
Bank	on deposit of cash or cheque	on withdrawal of cash on payment by cheque
Debtor's account	with credit sales when correcting undercharge when cheque dishonoured	when they pay when allowed a discount when goods are returned on correcting overcharge when given allowance with bad debt written off
Creditor's account	when they are paid on discount received when goods are returned on receipt of allowance when correcting overcharge	when bought from on correcting undercharge with cheque dishonoured
Current liabilities	when they are paid	when they are aquired
Long-term liabilities	on repayment	when borrowed
Capital account	with drawings with net loss	with investments with net profit
Income account	with income in advance(adj)	on receipt of income with an income due [adj]
Expense account	on payment with expense due [adj]	with expense in advance [adj]

ACCOUNT	WHEN IS IT DEBITED	WHEN IS IT CREDITED
Drawings account	when proprietor takes goods or cash	
Sales	with sales returns	with stock sales
Sales returns	with sales returns	
Purchases	with stock purchases	with purchases returns
Purchases returns		with purchases returns

11.6   The Ledger's Importance

1. That is where all transactions are finally recorded. .

2. It's the book where all accounts in the business are found.

3. It's the source of all balances used to prepare the trial balance, the profit and loss account, and the balance sheet.

Multiple Choice and Short Answer Questions

1. The section of the ledger where we find accounts that do not fit in any other section is

A. General ledger   B. Private ledger
C. Debtors ledger   D. Creditor's ledger

2. Which of the following is not recorded in the general ledger?

A. Fixed assets   B. Stock
C. Long term liabilities   D. Creditors

3. Debiting a givers account .... the balance on the account.

A. Increases   B. Reduces
C. Doesn't affect   D. Slightly affects

4. To increase the balance on a giving account we must.......... ....

A. Debit it   B. Credit it
C. Cancel it   D. None of these.

5. Unsatisfactory goods returned to the supplier are recorded on ....

A. Sales account   B. Purchases returns account
C. Purchases account   D. Sales returns account

6. Which of these accounts can have a positive or negative balance?

A. Cash account   B. Fixed asset
C. Current liability   D. Bank account

7. Stock not sold by the end of a period is referred to as

A. Opening stock   B. Stock at start
C. Closing stock   D. Stock taking

8. All the following are debit balance accounts except

A. Fixed assets   B. Current assets
C. Drawings   D. Current liabilities

9. When a loan is repaid by cheque we

Debit	Credit	Debit	Credit
A. Bank	Loan	B. Loan	Cash
C. Cash	Loan	D. Loan	Bank

10. Which of the following is not a credit balance account?

A. Drawings   B. Capital   C. Liabilities   D. Incomes

11.   Accounts for debtors are recorded in the

A. General ledger   B. Purchases ledger
C. Sales ledger   D. Cashbook

12.   Creditor's accounts are found in the

A. Purchases ledger   B. Sales ledger
C. General ledger   D. Nominal ledger

13. Draw a table to show what is recorded on the debit and credit sides of the following accounts; drawings, capital, stock, current assets, fixed assets, liabilities, income and expense accounts.

14. Describe the different types of accounts.

PPQ 1996

2. Complete the following table by showing the accounts to be debited and those to be credited

	Accounts to be credited	Accounts to be debited
i. Sold surplus stationery, receiving proceeds in cash		
ii. Commission received by us previously in error; we now refund this by cheque		
iii. Withdrew goods from the business for private use		
iv. A debt owing to us by bill of 68 is written off as a bad debt		
v. Rent received for premises sub-let by cheque		[10]

PPQ 1995

5B Complete the following table, showing the account to be debited and those to be credited

	Dr	Cr
i] sold second hand Motor van for cash		
ii] Bought stationery by cheque		
iii] Withdrew cash for personal use		
iv] Rent received by cheque		
v] Refund by cheque of insurance previously paid		

PPQ 1994

6. Enter the following transactions in appropriate subsidiary books, post to the ledger and balance the accounts for 1994.

July 1   credit purchases from K. Hlubi 380; M. Nyawo 500;
July 3   Credit sales to: E. Phakathi 246; F. Thikazi 356.
July 4   returns outwards M. Nyawo 30;
July 7   credit sales to: A. Gamedze 307; H. Ginindza 250
July 12 Returns inwards from: E. Phakatsi E18; F. Thikazi 22.

CHAPTER 12

TRIAL BALANCE AND SUSPENSE ACCOUNT

12.1   Trial Balance Uses

i). The most important use of a trial balance is to **ensure that double entry was done properly**. If there is any transaction recorded only once then the two totals will not be the same. That is how the trial balance exposes errors and we can have them corrected.

ii). The trial balance is used to **check the accuracy of additions and subtractions** done during the balancing of accounts. If they were not balanced properly then the totals will be different and this error is exposed. The additions on the trial balance itself should also be correct otherwise they are exposed.

12.2   Trial Balance Limitations

The trial balance was set up to expose errors that affect double entry and the balancing in the ledger. This includes wrong additions and subtractions, single entries, debiting or crediting twice, and others. If an error doesn't affect double entry and balancing then it can't be exposed by the trial balance. Not being able to expose all errors is what we refer to as its **limitations.**

An error is not recording correctly. Errors that can't be exposed by the trial balance include; error of principle, error of original entry, error of omission, error of commission, complete reversal of entries, and compensating errors. Below is an explanation for each of these errors and how they are corrected using journal entries and posting to the ledger.

12.3   Error of Omission

The word omission means not recorded anywhere. So this is an error where a transaction is not recorded in a subsidiary book or the ledger. This could be because the source document was skipped by error, or it was missing at the time of recording. This error can't be exposed since the debit and credit totals of the trial balance are both lacking the figure and they balance.

All kinds of omitted transactions are recorded for the first time in the general journal and they use it as their subsidiary book. For example, if a receipt for buying furniture by cheque was not recorded by error, we include it in the accounts starting with a journal entry as illustrated below;

Furniture	800	
Bank		800
Receipt was omitted		

This journal entry is posted by debiting the Furniture Account and crediting the Bank account as illustrated below;

Furniture Account

| Bank | 800 | |

Bank Account

| | | Furniture | 800 |

When the journal entry is posted to the ledger, the balance on the Furniture account increases by $800 and the balance on the Bank account reduces by $800. We should imagine there are other transactions on each of these accounts. Please note that we have written the bank account in the ledger and not the cashbook.

12.4   Error of Original Entry

This is an error which starts in the books of original entry (subsidiary books) and is posted to the ledger in error form. For example, an invoice of $200 to Joel a debtor is recorded in the sales journal as $20. The trial balance can't expose it because the debit and credit entries are both $20. All the trial balance does is to ensure the wrong figure satisfies double entry and there is proper balancing.

This is corrected by adding the difference of $180(200 -20) to the affected accounts using a journal entry as illustrated below;

Joel	180	
Sales		180
Invoice for 200 recorded as 20 by error		

This is posted to the ledger by debiting the Joel account and crediting the sales account as illustrated below;

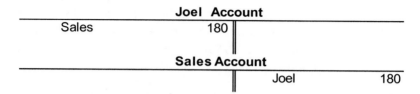

Joel Account

Sales	180	

Sales Account

	Joel	180

The balance on the Joel account increase by $180 to bridge the gap between $20 and $2000. The sales account balance also increases by $180.

12. 5   Complete Reversal of Entries

This is an error where the amount is posted to the correct accounts but on the wrong sides. For example, the sale of unwanted equipment for a cheque of $400. Posted by debiting the equipment account, and crediting the bank account.

This error can't be exposed because all the trial balance understands is that a transaction should be debited and credited, irrespective of whether these entries are on the correct accounts or the correct sides. So an error of debiting instead of crediting, and vice versa for the same transaction can't be exposed.

This is corrected by doubling the amounts (400 x 2) and recording on the correct (opposite) sides starting with a journal entry as illustrated below;

Bank	800	
Equipment		800
Complete reversal of entries		

This is posted to the ledger by debiting the Bank account and crediting the Equipment account as illustrated below;

Bank Account

Equipment	800	

Equipment Account

	Bank	800

The balance on the Bank account rises by only $400 and not $800. The reason for this is that the 1st $400 just reverses the error. It's the second $400 that increases the balance. The effect on the equipment account is similar.

12. 6   Error of Principle

This is an error where a transaction is recorded on an account which belongs to a different classification of accounts (Section 11.4). For example, the purchase of an asset being debited to the purchases account is an error, although the credit entry in the cash book is correct. The asset account which should have been debited is a real account, and yet the purchases account is an expense or nominal account.

The double entry requirement which could have been exposed by the trial balance is satisfied since there is a debit entry on the purchases account and a credit entry in the cashbook. If balancing on the two accounts is done properly then this error can't be exposed by the trial balance. The problem here lies with the purchases account which was debited, and the asset account which was not debited, but not the trial balance totals.

Another example is a bookshelf bought for $620 and debited to the purchases account by error. The correction is started with a journal entry which is illustrated below;

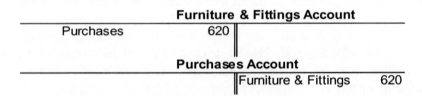

	Furniture and Fittings	620	
	Purchases		620
	Purchases debited by error		

This is posted to the ledger by debiting the furniture and fittings, and crediting the purchases account as illustrated below;

Furniture & Fittings Account

| Purchases | 620 |

Purchases Account

| | Furniture & Fittings | 620 |

The balance on the furniture and fittings account increases by $620, while the purchases balance reduces by $620.

12. 7   Error of Commission

This is an error where an entry is posted to the wrong account although both the correct and wrong accounts lie in the same class of accounts, like real or nominal accounts. For example, debiting Nick with goods for $350 instead of Nicholas and both are debtors. The debit entry is made on the Nick account instead of Nicholas account. The double entry requirement is satisfied and the trial balance totals agree.

The problem lies with Nick's account having an entry of what they didn't buy and their balance or debt is overstated, while Nicholas' balance or debt is understated. Both of them are personal accounts or debtors.

This is corrected by debiting Nicholas and crediting Nick with the amount, plus a narration. The correcting journal entry is illustrated below;

Nicholas	350	
Nick		350
Account debited by error		

This is posted by debiting the Nicholas account and crediting Nick's account as illustrated below;

Nicholas Account

Nick	350		

Nick Account

		Nicholas	350

After posting, the balance on the Nicholas account increases by $350, while the balance on the Nick account reduces by $350.

12. 8   Compensating Errors

This is a coincidence of a debit and a credit error, of equal amounts but on different accounts in the ledger. They increase or decrease both the debit and credit totals of the trial balance by the same amount and that's why they can't be exposed. For example, an account with a debit balance like stationery is over added by $15, and an account with a credit balance like commission earned is over added by $15. This coincidence can't be exposed by the trial balance since both the debit and credit totals on the trial balance contain an extra $15 by error.

This is corrected by recording the over added amount on the side opposite to the account's balance. Commission earned has a credit balance which is overstated. It's reduced by debiting it with the $15. Stationery which has an overstated debit balance is reduced by crediting it as illustrated by the journal entry below;

Commission Earned	15	
Stationery		15
Compensating errors of over adding		

This is posted by debiting the Commission earned and crediting Stationery account as illustrated below;

Commission Earned Account

Stationery	15	Income	180
To P & L	165		
	180		180

StationeryAccount

Expense	120	Nicholas	15
		To P & L	105
	120		120

After posting, the income on the Commission earned account falls by $15, while the expense on the Stationery account reduces by $15. So the amounts transferred to the profit and loss account are less.

However, if these errors are not teamed and corrected together, handling each one separately requires the use of the suspense account which provides the second entry. Please note that compensating errors are rare.

12. 9   The Suspense Account

The trial balance is only able to expose errors that affect double entry and the mathematical accuracy in the ledger. They include; **an overcast, undercast, single entries, crediting twice, debiting twice, debiting or crediting by error**, and others. This kind of errors are corrected using the suspense account.

A Suspense Account is an account used for correcting errors exposed by the trial balance. The errors are exposed when the trial balance totals are different. It's the difference between the two trial balance totals that calls for the use of the suspense account. If the trial balance balances then we don't need the suspense account.

The presence of a difference means there are errors and we need to find out where they are. When we open a suspense account, the figure we record first is the difference between the two totals. However, what happens with the correction procedure using the suspense account is beyond the coverage of this book. Please note, errors not exposed by the trial balance are not corrected using the suspense account.

Multiple Choice and Short Answer Questions

1. Which of the following errors is exposed by the trial   balance?

A   error of omission   B   error of principle
C   error of commission   D   Single entry

2. Which of the following does not appear on ledger accounts

A error of omission   B   error of commission
C error of principle   D   error of original entry

3. Which of the following errors is not   exposed by the trial balance?

A error of original entry   B   compensating error
C error of principal   D   all the above.

4. One   of the uses of a   trial balance is to

A identify   transactions   omitted   B ensure   double entry
C show   the financial   position   D show   the gross profit.

   Answer true or false to each of the statements below.

5. A trial balance is a list of company assets and liabilities.

6. When a trial balance balances it means there are no errors in the books of
   accounts.

7. The trial balance will still balance if motor expenses of $50 are debited to
   motor vehicles account.

8. Errors of omission do not affect the trial balance.

9.When an asset sold is recorded as stock sold then it's an error of principle.

10. Explain each of the following; [a] error of principle

[b] error of omission   [c] error of commission
[d] Compensating error   [e] error of original entry
[f] Complete reversal of entries

PPQ 2005
3. (a) The following Trial balance of Mandlakhe Spaza Phone for the month ending 30 April 2004 was prepared by an inexperienced bookkeeper.

Trial Balance for the month ended 30 April 2004

	Dr	Cr
Capital		1000
Sales	450	
Purcahses	300	
Cash in hand	10	
Cash at bank		260
Wages	60	
Advertising	75	
Equipment	525	
Stock 1 April (units)		150
Drawings		40
Rent and Rates	30	
	1450	**1450**

Required: Prepare a corrected Trial Balance. (Do not open ledger accounts) (12)

(b) List three errors which may not be detected by a trial balance. (3)

PPQ 2002
6. (a) Find below balances from the ledger of Roberts and Associates, from which you are required to prepare a trial balance as at 31 June 2001

Stationery	200	Capital	100,000
Insurance	350	Equipment	5,500
Sales	34,300	Electricity	345
Machinery	8,000	Rent	2,100
Credit & Cash purchases	42,500	Wages	900
Closing stock	3,870	Bank overdraft	2,735
Motor vehicles	45,000	Commission earned	165
		Water	135

PPQ 2001

5. From the following balances extracted from the books of
W. Phuphuma a trader, you are asked to prepare a trial balance as
at 30th June, 2000.

Capital	1,500	Insurance	67
Buildings	1,200	Rent receivable	55
Sales	5,250	General expenses	163
Purchases	3,820	Creditors	612
Returns inwards	75	Debtors	1,710
Returns outwards	35	Drawings	150
Carriage	57	Cash in hand	6
Discount received	87	Bank overdraft	194
Discount allowed	120	Repairs	72
Wages	365	Commission earned	250
		Electricity	178

PPQ 1999

6. From the following balances extracted from the books of Moses
Motsa at 31st December 1996, **draw** up his trial balance.

Capital	3,000	Discount Received	160
Premises	1,500	Wages	730
Fixtures and fittings	500	Insurance and Rates	135
Equipment	400	Rent Receivable	110
Sales	10,500	Sundry Expenses	325
Purchases	7,640	Creditors	1,224
Returns Inwards	150	Debtors	3,420
Returns Outwards	70	Cash in hand	12
Discount Allowed	240	Overdraft	288

PPQ 1998

6.a) Name, briefly explain and give relevant examples of 3 errors
that do not affect the Trial Balance Agreement.
          (9)

b) Show the journal entries necessary to correct the following errors:
i). A sale of goods 680 to S. Motsa has been entered in S. Matse's
account.
ii). The purchase of a sewing machinery from Skokwane Pty Ltd for
1,200 had been completely omitted from their books.
iii). The purchase of a motor van 9,500 had been entered in error
in the motor expenses account.
iv). A purchase of goods 200 had been entered in error on the debit
side of the drawings account.
          (11)

ADJUSTMENTS

13.1   Introduction

Adjustments are additions and subtractions made to ledger account balances in order to get the correct figures for the income statement. Adjustments are necessary because we need **accrued income** not income received, and **accrued expense** not expense paid. We use accrued incomes whether they are all received or not, and accrued expenses whether they are all paid or not. The word accrual and accrued come from accrue, which means to **increase.** Therefore, the profit and loss account requires figures that increased the incomes and expenses, in order to reveal the profit or loss for the period.

13.2   Purchases And Sales Adjustments

The selling price is got by adding a mark-up to the total cost of purchases. The total cost of purchases is got by adding direct expenses to the purchase cost. **Direct expenses on purchases** include transport (carriage inwards), taxes, insurance, and others.

Adjustments can be made directly to the purchases account in the ledger. Direct expenses are debited to the purchases account, while stock drawings, donations, and purchases returns are credited. When the account is balanced, the figure transferred to the Trading account is net purchases as illustrated below;

Purchases Account

2	Bank	350	31	Returns	183
25	Carriage inwards	140	31	To Trading A/c (Net purchases)	3,627
28	Taxes	335			
31	Creditors	2,985			
		3,810			3,810

This is net purchases and doesn't need any further adjustment on the Trading account.

Alternatively, this adjustment can be done on the Trading account. Direct expenses are added to the purchase price, and then we deduct purchases returns, stock drawings, and donations before we get net purchases as illustrated below;

THE TRADING ACCOUNT			
Sales			4,090
Sales Returns			- 231
Net Sales /Turnover			3,859
Opening Stock		325	
Purchases (350 + 2,985)	3,335		
Carriage Inwards	140		
Taxes	+ 335		
Gross Purchases	3,810		
Purchases Returns	- 183		
Net Purchases		+ 3,627	
Goods available for Sale		3,952	
Closing Stock		- 350	
Cost of Sales			- 3,602
Gross Profit			257

The only adjustment made on the sales figure is deducting sales returns to get Net sales/**Turnover** as illustrated above. However, sales returns can be debited to the sales account as illustrated below;

Sales Account				
30	Returns	231	5 Cash	320
	To Trading a/c (Net sales)	3,859	30 Debtors	3,770
		4,090		4,090

Balancing this account gives net sales, which is transferred to the Trading account, and no more adjustment to sales is necessary.

*EX 13A. You are **required** to make adjustments on the following accounts*
[i] The balance on the purchases account was 2,870 and returns was 182
[ii] The balance on sales account was 3,620 and sales returns was 230

EX 13B.   Gordon had the following balances from his trial balance; purchases - 2,870, closing stock - 585, sales returns - 184, carriage inwards -136, sales 3,965 opening stock - 280, taxes - 260, purchases returns -150.
*You are **required** to compile his trading account showing the adjustments*

13.3   Expense Paid And Expense Incurred

Expense paid is the actual amount given away for an expense. This is what appears on an expense account and trial balance.

The word **incur** refers to the outcome or result of an activity. Our focus is on business activity. So **expense incurred** refers to expenses resulting from business activities. If the business activity wasn't there, the expenses wouldn't arise. Therefore, an expense incurred is not what was paid, but what should be paid. Another term for expense incurred is **accrued expense**. The word **accrued** means increased. So, accrued expense refers to the increase in expenses for the period whether they are paid for or not.

When preparing the profit and loss account, we use the expense incurred and not the expense paid. In order to convert an expense paid to an expense incurred, an adjustment is done. Differences between an expense paid and expense incurred lead to either an **expense due** or an **expense in advance**.

13.4   Expense Due

This is the portion of expense incurred that is not yet paid. It arises when the **expense incurred is higher than the expense paid.** Since it's not yet paid, it doesn't appear on the ledger account. It only gets there through an adjustment that starts with a journal entry.

For example, the annual rent is $9,500 and yet the amount paid by year end is only $5,000. This means that $4,500 is outstanding. So the expense paid and showed by the ledger account is only $5,000, yet the expense incurred and required for the profit and loss account is $9,500. The adjustment starts with the following journal entry;

Rent	4,500	
Expenses Due		4,500
Amount outstanding		

We post this by **crediting expenses due** and debiting rent account as illustrated below.

Rent Paid Account

Bank(expense paid)	5,000	To P& L a/c (expense incurred)	9,500
Expense due (bal) c/d	**4,500**		
	9,500		9,500
		Expense due (balance) b/d	4,500

So the adjustment raises the rent balance to the incurred expense of $9,500 and that is what we use on the profit and loss account.

This adjustment can be done straight on the profit and loss account as illustrated below;

The Profit and Loss Account

Gross Profit			20,540
Interest Earned			+ 2,270
Total Income			22,810
Expenses			
Carriage Outwards		470	
Rent Paid	5,000		
Expense Due	**+ 4,500**		
		9,500	
Telephone		1,290	
Sundry Expenses		2,000	
Electricity	1,500		
Expense in Advance	**- 300**		
		+ 1,200	
Total Expenses			- 14,460
Net Profit			**8,350**

The expense due is added to the expense paid to get the rent expense incurred, and that is what we add to the other business expenses.

Below are some formulae based on expense due;

expense due = expense incurred – expense paid

expense incurred = expense paid + expense due

expense paid = expense incurred – expense due

The journal entry above, led to opening and crediting the expenses due account and its left with a credit balance as illustrated below;

Expenses Due Account

	Rent	4,500

Since this amount is owed, it's a current liability and it's recorded on the balance sheet as illustrated below;

BALANCE SHEET Extract		
Fixed Assets		
Motor vehicles		142,000
Furniture and fittings		+ 52,000
Total Fixed Aseets		194,000
Current Assets		
Stock	4,800	
Debtors	28,500	
Income Due (Commission)	1000	
Expense in Advance (Electricity)	300	
Cash	+ 3,700	
Total Current Aseets	38,300	
Current liabilities		
Creditors	17,350	
Bank Overdraft	5,000	
Income in Advance (Rent)	400	
Expense Due (Rent)	+ 4,500	
Total Current Liabilities		- 27,250
Net Current Assets		+ 11,050
Net Assets		205,050

13.5   Expense In Advance

This is an expense paid before it's incurred. It arises when the **expense paid is higher than the expense incurred,** and the difference is the expense in advance. For example, if the annual electricity bill is $1,200 (the expense incurred), and the business paid $1,500 (the expense paid), the **extra amount** of $300 is an **expense in advance**. It's commonly referred to as **a pre-payment**.

To reduce the amount paid on the account to the expense incurred that we require for the profit and loss account, an adjustment has to be made. It starts with the following journal entry;

Prepayments	300	
Electricity		300
Expense in advance		

This is posted by **debiting the prepayments account** and crediting the Electricity account as illustrated below;

Electricity Account

Cash(expense paid)	1,500	To P & L a/c (expense incurred)	1,200
		expense in advance (bal) c/d	300
	1,500		1,500
Prepayment b/d	300		

This adjustment reduces the amount paid to the expense incurred of $1,200 that we use on the profit and loss account.

This adjustment can be made on the profit and loss account. We deduct the expense in advance from the expense paid to get the expense incurred, which is added to the other business expenses. This is illustrated on the profit and loss account on page 134.

Below are some formulae based on expense in advance;
Expense in advance = expense paid – expense incurred

expense incurred = expense paid – expense in advance

Expense paid = expense incurred + expense in advance

The journal entry above, led to opening and debiting the prepayments account and its left with a debit balance as illustrated below;

Prepayments Account

Electricity	300	

The electricity company owes this prepayment and it's a **current asset** to the business. It's recorded on the balance sheet as illustrated above.

EX 13C. A business paid $400 to an insurance company. However, they later discovered that only $360 was needed for that period. You are required to compile the insurance account showing the insurance expense transferred to the profit and loss account, and the expense in advance brought down.

13.6   Stationery Stock

Stationery is an expense and it's written off to the profit and loss account at the end of a trading period. However, stationery **not used** by the end remains as stationery stock. It's like any other **expense paid in advance**. Therefore, some adjustment is necessary to show the value of stationery used and transferred to the profit and loss account, and the value carried down to the following period as stationery stock.

For example, if the amount paid for stationery is $85 and a value of $20 is not used by the end. The amount actually spent on stationery and used for the period is; 85 - 20 = $65, and that is the **stationery expense**. It's wrong to record $85 on the profit and loss account when stationery for $20 was not used. The stationery account is adjusted as follows;

Stationery Account

Bank (payment)	85	To profit and loss A/c	65
		(Stationery stock) Balance c/d	20
	85		85
(Stationery stock) Balance b/d	20		

Stationery stock is a current asset since it's **physically available** by the end of the period. It's recorded as a prepayment, among the **current assets** on the balance sheet. It becomes an expense when it's used in the following period and that is when it's transferred to the profit and loss account.

13.7   Income Received And Income Earned

Income received is the amount of money **receipted** by the cashier in a business. This is what appears on the income account and trial balance.

Income earned is the amount of money **worked for** by selling goods and services. It's also known as **Accrued income**, which refers to the increase in income during the period. The business could have received some and part of it is not received by the end of the period. For example, the business could have done some work and it's entitled to a commission of $6,000. The business may have received only $4,500 leaving a balance of $1,500. The **income received** and **showed** by the income account is only $4,500, yet the income earned or worked for is $6,000. Because the profit and loss account uses the income earned and not income received, an adjustment has to be made. Differences between income received and income earned lead to either an **income due** or an **income in advance**.

13.8   Income Due

This is income worked for but is not yet received by the end of a period. The **income received is less than income earned** and the difference is the income due. For example, it may have received only $3,600 for commission and yet the total is supposed to be $4,600. So the balance of $1,000 is an income due. The income earned is $4,600 although the income account and trial balance only show $3,600. This amount has to be adjusted to income earned that is required for the profit and loss account. This adjustment is started with a journal entry as illustrated below;

Income Due	1,000	
Commission Received		1,000
Income not received		

This is posted by **debiting the Income Due account** and crediting the Commission Received account as illustrated below;

Commission Received Account

(Income Earned) To P & L a/c	4,600	Bank (Income received)	3,600
		Income due (bal) c/d	1,000
	4,600		4,600
Income due (bal) b/d	1,000		

When the $1,000 is added to $3,600, we get the income earned required for the profit and loss account. This adjustment can be done on the profit and loss account as illustrated below;

A Profit and Loss Account (extract)		
Gross Profit		24,800
Rent Received	3,500	
Income in Advance	**- 400**	
Rent Income Earned		3,100
Commission Received	3,600	
Income due	**+ 1,000**	
Commission Earned		+ 4,600
Total Income		32,500
Expenses		
Insurance	1,200	
Rent Paid	3,500	
continues below		

The income due is added to income received to get the income earned.

The journal entry above, led to debiting the income due account and its left with a debit balance as illustrated below;

Income Due Account

Commission Earned	1,000	

Whoever hasn't paid the $1,000 owes and is a debtor to the business. This is a **current asset** and is recorded next to other debtors on the balance sheet as illustrated on page 135.

Below are some formulae based on income due;
Income Due = Income earned – Income Received.

Income Received = Income earned – Income Due

Income earned = Income Received + Income Due

EX 13D.
A business was renting out part of its building for $800 per month. It had received $580 by the end of the month. You are required to calculate its rent income due, and show the amount transferred to the profit and loss account.

13.9   Income In Advance

This is income received before it's worked for. The **income received is more than the income earned** and the difference is the income in advance. That means that some of the income received does not belong to the present but the following period. For example, a business rents out part of its premises at $3,100 per month. If the sub-letters paid $3,500, this means an extra $400. The $3,500 is income received, the $3,100 is income earned, and income in advance is $400.

The rent received account and trial balance show 3,500 and this has to be adjusted to the period's income by deducting the income in advance. This is started with a journal entry as illustrated below;

Rent Received	400	
Income in Advance		400
Income not yet earned		

This is posted by **crediting the Income in Advance account** and debiting the Rent Received account as illustrated below;

Rent Received

(Income earned) To P & L A/c	3,100	Cash (income received)	3,500
Income in advance (bal) c/d	400		
	3,500		3,500
		Income in advance (bal) b/d	400

This entry reduces $3,500 to $3,100 that is the income for the period. This adjustment can be done on the profit and loss account as illustrated on the previous page. The income in advance is deducted from income received to get income earned. That is what we add to gross profit and other incomes to get total income.

Below are some formulae based on income in advance;
Income in advance = Income Received − Accrued Earned

Income earned = Income Received − Income in advance

Income Received = Income in advance + Income Earned

The journal entry above, led to crediting the Income in Advance account and its left with a credit balance as illustrated below;

Income In Advance Account

	Rent Received	400

All cash received in advance is owed and remains a **current liability** until it's earned. So it's recorded on the balance sheet next to the other creditors as illustrated on page 135.

EX 13E *According to Tina's trading account the gross profit was 1,890, the other incomes were; interest received - 148, discount received - 106, the expenses were; rent paid - 340, wages - 550, discount allowed - 89,*
bank charges - 32 and stationery - 85
The adjustments to be made were; interest income due - 25, rent due - 260, and stationary stock - 32
*You are **required** to prepare her profit and loss account showing the adjustments*

Below is a summarised table for some adjustment procedure;

	Profit & Loss A/c Treatment	Balance Sheet Treatment
income due	add to trial balance figure	current asset
income in advance	deduct from trial balance figure	current liability
expense due	add to trial balance figure	current liability
expense in advance	deduct from trial balance figure	current asset
Stationery stock	deduct from stationery expense	current asset

Adjustments for bad debts and depreciation are explained in the following chapter.

13.10   Capital And Revenue Income

The money received by a business may be classified as a capital income or revenue income.

Capital Income: This is money received and it increases the capital in a business. It refers to the non-trading sources of income towards capital, and the long term

liabilities like a bank loan. So it's mainly the owner's contributions towards capital, and the borrowed capital. We can say that capital income doesn't really belong to the business since capital is also a liability.

Revenue Income: This is money generated by the business through its trading activities like the selling of goods and provision of services. This includes sales, rent received, commission earned, interest received, and others. This is what leads to **profit** in a business.

The lines of distinction is **capital growth and ownership**. If an income leads to an increase in capital then it's a capital income, and if it does not then it's a revenue income. If it belongs to the business then it's a revenue income and if it doesn't then it's a capital income.

Both types of income can eventually turn into cash or bank at some point. It isn't necessary knowing what type of income it is before you use it to buy an asset, or pay for an expense. All we know is that its income we use to buy and increase assets, and pay for expenses.

It's from the revenue income that we get the **profit** in the business. From revenue income we deduct the cost of sales, deduct the expenses and what is left is profit.

13.11   Capital And Revenue Expenditure
The money spent by a business can be classified as capital or revenue expenditure.

Capital Expenditure: This is money spent on buying, constructing or adding value to fixed assets. The cost of a fixed asset includes all the expenses incurred in bringing it into a working condition. This includes the buying, transportation, taxes and installation costs. Money spent on **increasing the value, or extending the life** of fixed assets is also regarded as a capital expenditure. Examples are; making extensions to a building, fitting an extra part to a machine, fitting a canopy to a bakkie, and others.

Revenue Expenditure: This is money spent on financing the day-to-day running expenses of the business or organisation. This includes rent paid, advertising, salaries & wages, insurance, and others. It's mainly to do with expenses and this includes purchases on the trading account. Expenses incurred to repair, maintain, or keep fixed assets in a working condition are also regarded as a revenue expenditure.

The major line of distinction between the two categories of expenditure is the period. The usage or benefit from a revenue expenditure does not normally exceed one year, whereas the benefit from a capital expenditure exceeds one year.

The purchase of a motor vehicle is a capital expenditure, whereas its maintenance (motor expenses) is a revenue expenditure.

The cost of buying a house is a capital expenditure, whereas the repairs and maintenance is a revenue expenditure.

The purchase of a machine is a capital expenditure, whereas its repair and maintenance costs are a revenue expenditure.

Capital expenditure is added to the value of fixed assets and it's recorded on the balance sheet. Revenue expenditure is what makes up the **expenses** recorded on the trading, profit and loss account.

Below is a summary of the differences;

Capital Expenditure	Revenue Expenditure
1 for fixed assets	for day to day running expenses
2 used for over one year	used for less than a year
3 increases the fixed assets value	increases the expenses
4 recorded on the balance sheet	recorded on the trading, profit and loss account

Multiple Choice and Short Answer Questions
1. Which of the following combinations is correct?

Current asset	Current liability		Current asset	Current liability
A. Income due	Prepayment		B. Income due	Expense due
C. Income due	Expense in advance		D. Expenses due	Income due

2. The monthly rent for a house is $1,500. If the rent paid is $1,350, what is the rent due?

A. 1,500   B. 1,350   C. 2,850   D. 150

3. On a balance sheet, unused stationery is treated as a
A. Fixed asset   B. Current asset
C. Current liability   D. Fixed liability

4. All the following are expenses except?
A. Stationery stock   B. Motor expenses
C. Insurance   D. Bank charges.

5. Stationery stock is an...
A. Income in advance   B. Expense in advance
C. Expense due   D. Expense outstanding

6. Income received less income earned equals

A. Income due   B. Income in advance
C. Prepayment   D. Amount received
7. Income received plus income due equals
A. Income earned   B. Income due
C. Income outstanding   D. Amount received
8. Which of the following expenses is transferred to the profit and loss account?
A. Prepayment   B. Expense in advance
C. Expense incurred   D. expense paid
9. Which one of the following is transferred to the profit and loss account?
A. Income due   B. Income in advance
C. Income outstanding   D. Income earned
10. Explain the differences between a capital expenditure and a revenue expenditure.
11. What are the differences between a revenue income and a revenue expenditure
12. Differentiate between the following;
[a] expense paid and expense incurred
[b] income earned and income received
[c] income in advance and income due
[d] expense in advance and expense due
13. Explain the adjustment made to the following;
[a] sales   [b] purchases   [c] stock
[d] stationery stock
14.   Arrange the following items in groups of **capital income**, **capital expenditure, revenue income and revenue expenditure;**
   motor vehicles, advertising, rent received, wages, salaries, capital, motor expenses, land, repairs and maintenance, commission earned, purchases, furniture, discount allowed, discount received, loan, interest on loan, and bank charges.

PPQ 2004
4. The following balances appear in the books of Bhekinkhosi Trading Store on December 31 2001.

Capital	1500-00	Purchases	10 000-00
Discount allowed	100-00	Discount Received	500-00
Sales	17000-00	Salaries	700-00
Opening Stock	1700-00	Insurance	500-00
Sales returns	1000-00	Stationery	450-00
Rent Received	100-00	Closing Stock	500-00

Required: Prepare a Trading, Profit and loss account for the year ending 31 December 2001.
Showing clearly the following:-
(1) Net sales   (2) Total purchases   (3) Gross profit
(4) Cost of goods sold (5) Total expenses   (6) Total income
(7) Net profit / loss

PPQ 2000

7. The following trial balance appeared in the books of C.Cebe a sole trader at the close of business on 31st May, 1999.

Sundry expenses	70	
Debtors and Creditors	770	530
Stock 1 June 1998	860	
Capital 1 June 1998		2,500
Drawings	650	
Purchases and Sales	2,340	4,110
Discounts	120	70
Cash	20	
Bank	640	
Wages and Salaries	950	
Equipment	370	
Carriage Outwards	220	
Rent and Rates	170	
Bad Debts	30	
	7,210	7,210

You are **required** to prepare the trading, profit and loss account for the year ending 31 May 1999 and a balance sheet as at that date.
a) Stock at 31 May 1990 1,090 Rand.
b) Rent and rates prepaid at 31st May 1999 R30.
c) Allow R40 depreciation on equipment.

PPQ 2003

1. The following balances are for Mazibonele Grocery for June 2000.

Gross profit	2054	Sundry expenses	200
Insurance	220	Carriage outwards	47
Rent	500	Bank charges	28
Interest earned	227	Electricity	150
Telephone	100		

You are required to prepare a Profit and Loss account, taking into account the following adjustments:
(i) Rent owing E450.   (ii) Electricity paid in advance E30.
(iii) Telephone due E29.

2b (i) Define the following:
Capital expenditure   Revenue expenditure
(ii) Give an example of a **capital** expense and a **revenue** expense

PPQ 1999

3. *The following trading, profit and loss account for the year ended 31st December 1984 was drawn up by an inexperienced Accounts Clerk for his employer who was an Office Stationery dealer:*

Trading, Profit and Loss Account as at 31st December, 1984

Discount Received			370	Sales	60,100
Rent and Rates	1,225			Less purchases	- 33,420	26,680
Add Prepayments	+ 200	1,425			
Wages and Salaries		15,500	Discount Allowed		420
Returns Inwards		270	Stock 1st Jan. 1984		2,900
Returns Outwards		430			
Carriage Outwards	1,100				
Less Carriage Inwards	- 900	200			
Purchase of Motor Van	5,000				
Less Depreciation	- 625	4,375			
Stock 31 Dec. 1984		3,240			
Net Profit		4,190			
		30,000			30,000

There are a number of errors and you are **required** *to re-write the Trading, Profit and Loss Account as it should be presented.*

PPQ 1997

5. *From the following trial balance of Majazana, draw up a trading and profit and loss account for the year ended 30 Sept 1997 and a balance sheet as at that date.*

	DEBIT	CREDIT
Stock 1 Oct. 1996	23,680	
Purchases	123,000	
Sales		188,330
Salaries	38,620	
Rent and Rates	5,000	
Insurance	780	
Motor Expenses	6,640	
Office Expenses	2,200	
Light and Heat	1,660	
General Expenses	3,140	
Premises	50,000	
Motor Vehicles	18,000	
Fixtures and fittings	3,500	
Debtors	38,960	
Creditors		17,310
Cash at Bank	4,820	
Drawings	12,000	
Capital	.	.126,360
	332,000	332,000

At 30 September 1997;
a] Stock   29,460
b] Rates owing   600
c] Insurance prepaid   120
d] Light and Heat expenses owing   320.

ANSWERS

13B   **Trading Account**

Sales			3,965
sales Returns			184
Net Sales			3,781
Opening Stock		280	
Purchases	2,870		
Carriage Inwards	136		
Taxes	260		
Gross Purchases	3,266		
Purchases Returns	150		
Net Purchases		3,116	
Goods available for Sale		3,396	
Closing Stock		585	
Cost of Sales			2,811
Gross Profit			970

CHAPTER   14

BAD DEBTS AND DEPRECIATION

14.1   Introduction

A bad debt is money which debtors have failed to pay and it's a loss. It arises from credit sales. In spite of improved credit control measures, some debtors still don't pay.   Some of the reasons for failure to pay are; dishonesty, bankruptcy, losses through theft and mismanagement, loss of jobs, death, and others. If all the debt collection tactics have failed and you are convinced the debtor(s) will not pay, the amount owed should be written off as a bad debt. The amount written off is transferred from the debtors account to the bad debts account.

This write off doesn't involve a movement of cash and is just an adjustment that closes the debtor's account. The subsidiary book is the **general journal**. In the journal entry the bad debts account is to be debited, while the bad debtor's account is to be credited, plus a narration as illustrated below;

Bad debts	175	
Debtor- Mark		175
Debt written off		

The journal entry is posted by debiting the bad debts account and crediting the debtor's account. This actually closes the debtor's account with no balance as illustrated below;

Mark (Debtor)

| 14.05.00 | Sales | 175 | 31.12.00 | Bad Debts | 175 |

Bad Debts Account

| 31.12.00 | Mark | 175 | 31.12.00 | To P & L | 175 |

This process is normally done at the end of a financial year just before preparing the final accounts.

14.2   Bad Debts And The Profit And Loss Account

A debt arises when a sale is made and it increases the total income. When it's written off it becomes a loss or an expense. Therefore, we reverse its impact by deducting it from total income (where it was added). It's initially transferred to the bad debts account as illustrated above. We then transfer all bad debts to the profit and loss account by listing them among the other expenses. They are deducted from total income as part of the total expenses. This is illustrated on the income statement below;

Jackson's Profit & Loss Account for the month ended 30 August 2003		
Gross Profit		26,315
x **Bad Debts Recovered**		**220**
Total Income		26,535
Operating Expenses		
Stationery	200	
Telephone	270	
Water	120	
x **Bad debts**	**175**	
Sundry expenses	64	
Total Expenses		829
Net Profit		**25,706**

14.3   Bad Debts And The Balance Sheet

If a Bad debt is written off before the year end, the account is closed and that debtor's balance is not part of the debtor's total on the balance sheet. No adjustment is necessary. The debtor's total is an addition of individual debtor's balances in the sales ledger. However, if the bad debt is written off after the year end when the debtor's total is already done, then it needs to be adjusted on the balance sheet as illustrated below;

Balance Sheet Extract		
Fixed Assets		
Motor vehicles		14,200
Furniture and fittings		+ 5,200
Total Fixed Aseets		19,400
Current Assets		
Stock		980
Debtors	**2,375**	
Bad debts	**- 175**	
Recoverable Debtors		2,200
Bank		430
Cash		+ 70
Total Current Assets		3,680

The individual debtor balance written off, **is deducted** from the debtor's total on the balance sheet. This leaves only the net realisable or recoverable debtors as illustrated above.

14.4 Bad Debts Recovered

A debt is only written off after the steps of recovering payment have failed. When a debt is written off, the debtor's account is closed and they are not allowed anymore credit. However, the business keeps a record of debts written off. If a bad debtor eventually pays, it's received as a bad debt recovered. The subsidiary book is the cashbook since it involves a receipt of cash. So the debit entry is in the cashbook and the credit entry is on the bad debts recovered account as illustrated below;

Bad Debts Recovered Account

To P & L	175	Cashbook (Mark)	175

The bad debts recovered account is an income account and it has a credit balance. The total of bad debts recovered is transferred to the profit and loss account, and added to gross profit as illustrated on previous page. It's not recorded on the balance sheet. Please note that bad debts written off is not the same as bad debts recovered. Below is a summary of the differences;

	Bad Debts	Bad Debts Recovered
1	An expense	An income
2	Reduces net profit	Increases net profit
3	Deducted on balance sheet	Not recorded on balance sheet
4	Both are recorded on the income statement	

EXERCISE 14A.
Write the following transactions in the general journal and post to the ledger. Narrations are required.
7th Took stock valued at $85 for personal use
13th A debtor named Felicity failed to pay her debt of $630 she was owing since last year, it was written off
21st A debt of $140 written off last year was recovered from Adrian in cheque form.

14.5 Doubtful Debts Provision

A doubtful debt is an amount of money that is suspected of not being paid by debtors. This money was initially recorded as sales and since it's not expected to be paid then it's better to reduce the sales figure. Instead of deducting it directly from sales, we group it with the other expenses to be deducted from the incomes.

A Provision is an amount of money set aside for a known expense, although the exact amount is not known. The aim of creating a provision is to avoid coming up with a high profit and later reducing it because a known expense had to be written off. So instead of writing off a guessed amount immediately on the income statement, we wait to confirm the amount and write it off using the provision created.

Therefore, **a doubtful debts provision** is an amount set aside to cater for debts that are suspected of not being paid. Through experience, businesses which sell on credit know that some debtors don't pay, what is not known is the exact amount of bad debts. It is also known as a **provision for bad debts.**

The amount of doubtful debts is derived as **a percentage of outstanding debtors** at the year end. This percentage is normally determined basing on experience of the previous years. If debtors that eventually became bad were 5% of outstanding debtors, then the business will set aside 5% of outstanding debtors at the year end. If they were 7% then the business will deduct 7% of the outstanding debtors from gross profit, and set it aside as a provision for doubtful debts.

For example; if outstanding debtors is $5,625 and the provision for bad debts is set at 4%, the amount set aside will be;

$$5,625 \times 4\% = 225$$

A doubtful debts provision is one of the adjustments done at the year end, before we can get a realistic net profit and a recoverable value of outstanding debtors. If the past shows that 5% do not pay then it is only prudent /sensible that we leave only 95% of outstanding debtors on the balance sheet. The provision for doubtful debts is deducted from gross profit and this leads to a lower but more realistic net profit. So the increase in owner's equity due to net profit is reduced by 5%. The Net Assets are also reduced by the same amount, by deducting the doubtful debts provision from the debtor's balance as illustrated in the following section.

This is based on the prudence concept (chapter 19) which says that all anticipated losses should be deducted before we get net profit. This is to ensure that the net profit we get does not have to be adjusted downwards later when a doubtful debt proves to be bad in a subsequent financial period.

14.6 Doubtful Debts Provision & Final Accounts

When a doubtful debts provision amount is derived, its first recorded in a journal entry as illustrated below;

Profit & Loss Account		225	
Provision for Bad Debts			225

It's then posted by **crediting** the provision for bad debts account as illustrated below;

Doubtful Debts Provision Account

Bad Debts	175	From Profit & Loss Account	225
Balance c/d	50		
	225		225
		Balance b/d	50

Once this provision is created, bad debts are not taken to the profit and loss account any more; they are instead transferred to the provision for bad debts account as illustrated here. For example, the bad debts of $175 is deducted from the provision of $225 created. The place for bad debts on the income statement is then occupied by the provision for bad debts as shown below. The only exception to this is in the year of creating the provision. During that year, we can have both bad debts and the provision for bad debts on the income statement. This is because the provision created is based on, and is for outstanding debts at the year end, and not debts already written off. In the years that follow, the provision set up should be enough to cover any eventual bad debts written off.

The debit entry is made on the profit and loss account by recording it among the expenses in the debit column as illustrated below;

Khama's Profit & Loss Account		
Gross Profit /Total Income		26,535
Operating Expenses		
Wages	3,200	
Rent Paid	2,400	
Stationery	200	
Telephone	270	
Discount Allowed	78	
Carriage outwards	220	
Transport	180	
Water	120	
x **Provision for Bad Debts**	**225**	
Sundry expenses	64	
Total Expenses		6,957
Net Profit		**19,578**

This provision is one of the items deducted from total income and it's treated as an expense.

This is where the provision amount comes from. The provision for bad debts account is not closed and it has a credit balance. It can be recorded among the current liabilities on the balance sheet. However, because of the need to show recoverable debtors on the balance sheet, we prefer to deduct this from outstanding debtors on the balance sheet. Since the bad debts end up on the provision for bad debts account, their place on the balance sheet is taken up by the provision as illustrated below;

Balance Sheet Extract		
Current Assets		
Stock		980
Debtors	2,375	
Provision for Bad Debts	- 225	
Recoverable Debtors		2,150
Bank		430
Cash		+ 70
Total Current Assets		3,630

14.7   Adjusting The Doubtful Debts Provision

Bad debts are written off using the credit balance on the doubtful debts provision account and this reduces its balance. In the illustration above, the provision of $225 was reduced to $50. However, the closing balance on this account is determined by the percentage of outstanding debtors suspected of not paying. For example, if debtors for the current year is $12,000, and you need 5% as a provision at the year end. The closing balance on the account should be $600 = (12,000 x 5%). Therefore, we have to upgrade the balance of $50 by getting another $550 from the profit and loss account. We debit the profit and loss account and credit this account as illustrated below;

Doubtful Debts Provision Account

Bad Debts	175	Balance b/d	225
Balance c/d	600	From P & L	550
	775		775
		Balance b/d	600

We get the $550 as the difference between the required balance of $600 and the available provision of $50.

     600 – 50 = 550.

So the closing balance of 600 is what we deduct from debtors on the balance sheet.

We now know that it's the percentage of outstanding debtors which determines the closing balance on this account. However, how much we get from the profit and loss account depends on; the bad debts written off, the opening balance, and the required closing balance on the provision account. The closing balance is added to bad debts and we deduct their total from the opening balance, to get what should come from the profit and loss account. According to the figures above, it's done as follows;

Bad debts	175
Required closing balance	+ 600
	775
Opening balance	- 225
More from P & L	550

If the answer is positive then the available provision is not enough. The positive amount is what we get from the profit and loss account and record it on the credit side of the account as illustrated above. If the answer is negative, it means the available provision is more than enough. So the excess negative amount has to be taken back to the profit and loss account by adding it to the other incomes.

For example, if debtors are $600 and the provision is 5%, the closing balance should be 30 (600 x 5%). If the opening balance or provision available is more than the required closing balance and the bad debts written off, then the excess should be taken back to the profit and loss account as illustrated below.

Bad debts	175
Required closing balance	+ 30
	205
Opening balance	225
Exces back to P & L	- 20

So the excess $20 is debited to the provision account as illustrated below;

Doubtful Debts Provision Account

Bad Debts	175	Balance b/d	225
Back to P & L	20		
Balance c/d	30		
	225		225
		Balance b/d	30

So the amount deducted or added back to the profit and loss account is the one for adjusting the balance to the required closing provision for bad debts.

The one deducted on the balance sheet is just a percentage of outstanding debtors.

14.8   Depreciation

Depreciation is the value of a fixed asset used up and written off to the profit and loss account. The easiest way of getting the depreciation figure is; dividing the asset cost by the number of years it's expected to be used. By this we are saying that depreciation is the cost of a fixed asset divided by the expected years of use. So the cost of the asset is allocated to the different years and written off as an expense. The reasoning is that an asset is used for many years and its huge cost can't be written off in the year of purchase. It's written off in the name of depreciation, as the asset is used and looses value.

A new asset has a higher value than one used for two years. The longer it's been used, the lower the value left in an asset since part of it is written off every year. However, whether an asset is used or not, it looses value.

Appreciation is the rise in the value of a fixed asset. Some assets like land do not lose value but instead gain. So they are not depreciated.

14.9   The Straight Line Method

The most common methods of calculating depreciation are the straight line and reducing balance.

The Straight Line is a method where a fixed amount is written off the value of an asset every year. The depreciation amount is either **a fixed percentage of the cost**, or we use the formula;

CP – RV   Where **CP** is the cost price of the asset
NY   **RV** is the residual value of the asset at the end of its use. This is normally the value of materials used to produce it.
                     NY is the number of years the asset is to be used.

By this method, the amount of depreciation written off is the same for all the years and that's why it's referred to as the **fixed instalment method**.

If the asset has no residual value then the formula is simply;

CP (cost price)
NY (number of years)

For example, if a machine is bought for $14,000 and its useful life is expected to be three years. If the residual value is to be $2,000, what is the annual depreciation?

$$\frac{(1,400 - 2,000)}{3} = 400$$

If we are to use a fixed percentage of 25% on a cost of 2,000 then the annual depreciation is;

2,000 x 25% = 500.
So we write off 500 every year and by the end of the fourth year, the total cost of 2,000 is all written off to the profit and loss account.

14.10 The Reducing Balance Method

Reducing balance is a method where the amount of depreciation is calculated as a percentage on cost or the net book value. **Net book value (NBV)** is the value left in an asset after deducting depreciation for the previous years. It is also known as the **written down value**.

In the **first year** the percentage is calculated on **cost** since the asset is not yet depreciated. For the following years it's calculated on the net book value, which is actually a **reduced balance** as compared to the one for the previous year. Since depreciation is calculated every year on the reducing balance, then we refer to this one as the **reducing balance method**.

For example, if the cost of an asset in 2002 was $1,000 and depreciation was 10% on the reducing balance. The calculations are;

1st year–10% on the cost price of $1,000 is $100 leaving a **NBV** of $900
2nd year –10% on the NBV of $900 is $90 leaving a NBV of $810
3rd year –10% on the NBV of $810 is $81 leaving a NBV of $729.
Calculations continue until the end of the useful period of the asset. This is presented clearly below;

1st year

cost	1,000
depreciation charge (10% on cost)	- 100
NBV at the end of 1st year	900
2nd year	
depreciation charge (10% on the NBV of 900)	- 90
NBV at the end of 2nd year	810
3rd year	
depreciation charge (10% on the NBV of 810)	- 81
NBV at the end of 3rd year	729

14.11   Recording Depreciation

The cost of all we use in a business is recorded on the profit and loss account as an expense. Because fixed assets are used for many years, their cost can't be written off in the year of purchase. Their cost is spread over the years of use and written off as depreciation. How much cost to write off each year is calculated by the straight line, reducing balance, or other method. This cost is normally written off at the end of the year.

After depreciation is calculated, its recorded starting with a journal entry as illustrated below;

Depreciation	100	
Equipment		100
10% depreciation on cost		

It's then posted to the debit side of a **depreciation account** that is created, and the credit side of the **asset account** as illustrated below;

Depreciation Account

Equipment	100	To P & L a/c	175
Furniture	75		
	175		175

Depreciation for all assets is recorded on the same account. The above account has depreciation for equipment and the furniture. The total on this account is transferred to the profit and loss account and recorded among the expenses as illustrated below;

The Profit and Loss Account		
Gross Profit		6,180
Expenses		
Rent paid	750	
Wages	800	
Advertising	87	
Insurance	325	
Depreciation :	**175**	
Total Expenses		2,137
Net Profit		**4,043**

Below is the equipment account credited with the above journal entry;

Equipment Account

Bank	1,000	Depreciation	100
		Balance c/d	900
	1,000		1,000
Balance b/d (NBV)	900		

When this account is balanced, we are left with **net book value**. This is the fixed assets value we add to net current assets to get the net assets on the balance sheet. However, if the calculation is not done on the asset account then we can do it straight on the balance sheet as illustrated below;

BALANCE SHEET Extract			
Fixed Assets	Cost	Depreciation	NBV
Motor Vehicles	1,000	100	900
Furniture and fittings	750	75	675
	1,750	175	1,575
Current Assets			
Stock		870	
Debtors		3,190	
Bank		1,450	
Cash		305	
TCA		5,815	
Current Liabilities			
Creditors	1,640		
TCL		1,640	
Net Current Assets			4,175
Net Assets			5,750

Depreciation is deducted from the cost of the asset to get the net book value.

EX 14B. *The following Trial Balance was extracted from the books of Fredric at the end of 2005.*

Cash	333	Capital	29,173
Stock	410	Bank overdraft	1,185
Buildings	39,400	Sales	48,250
Furniture	4,100	Rent income	3,000
Machinery	2,300	Discount received	317
Drawings	1,200	Purchases returns	574
Repairs	520		
Water	330		
Wages	2,700		
Purchases	26,150		
Sales returns	630		
Insurance	450		
Stationary	220		
Sundry expenses	160		
Debtors	3,310		
Discounts allowed	286		
	82,499		82,499

Adjustments

1. *Closing stock was $250*
2. *Bad debts of $290 were to be written off*
3. *$600 was due from tenants by the end of the year*
4. *$80 was due for repairs*
5. *$30 had been paid in advance for insurance*
6. *Furniture was to be depreciated by 6%*
7. *Machinery was to be depreciated by 10%*

*You are **required** to:- i) write his trading, profit and loss account, ii) prepare a balance sheet showing the adjustments.*

Multiple Choice and Short Answer Questions

1. Which of the following combinations is correct?

Current asset	Current liability		Current asset	Current liability
A. Income due	Prepayment		B. Income due	Expense due
C. Income due	Expense in advance		D. Expenses due	Income due

2. The monthly rent for a house is $1,500. If the rent paid is $1,350, what is the rent due?

A. 1,500   B. 1,350   C. 2,850   D. 150

3. On a balance sheet, unused stationery is treated as a

A. Fixed asset   B. Current asset
C. Current liability   D. Fixed liability

4. The entries for writing off a bad debt are:

	Debit	Credit		Debit	Credit
A.	Debtors	Bad debts		B. Creditors	Bad debts
C.	Bad debts	Creditors		D. Bad debts	Debtors

5. Stationery stock is an...

A. Income in advance   B. Expense in advance
C. Expense due   D. Expense outstanding

6. Income received less income earned equals

A. Income due   B. Income in advance

C. Prepayment   D. Amount received

7. Income received plus income due equals
A. Income earned   B. Income due
C. Income outstanding   D. Amount received

8. Which of the following expenses is transferred to the profit and loss account?
A. Prepayment   B. Expense in advance
C. Expense incurred   D. expense paid

9. Which one of the following is transferred to the profit and loss account?
A. Income due   B. Income in advance
C. Income outstanding   D. Income earned

10. All the following are expenses except?
A. Stationery stock   B. Motor expenses
C. Insurance   D. Bank charges.

11. When preparing final accounts the balance on the bad debts account is transferred to the?
A. Profit and Loss Account   B. Trading Account
C. Debtor's Account   D. Creditor's Account

12. To get recoverable debtors we have to deduct bad debts from
A. Balance sheet   B. Creditors
C. Bad debts   D. Debtors

13. The entries for a bad debt recovered are;

Debit	Credit	Debit	Credit
A. Cashbook	Debtors	B. Cashbook	Bad debts
C. Bad debts	Cashbook	D. Cashbook	Bad debts recovered

14. Depreciation is the
A. Cost of replacing an asset.   B. Money put aside to replace the asset.
C. The loss in the value of an asset.   D. None of these

15. The amount of depreciation is recorded by:

Debit	Credit	Debit	Credit
A. Depreciation	Asset	B. Asset	Profit and loss
C. Depreciation	Profit and loss	D. None of these	

16. The value of fixed assets considered on the balance sheet is:
A. Cost   B. Net Book Value
C. Depreciation   D. Replacement Cost

17. Depreciation is recorded in the same subsiding book as:
A. Purchases   B. Sales
C. Cheques   D. Stock Drawings

18. Differentiate between the following;
[a] expense paid and expense incurred
[b] income earned and income received
[c] income in advance and income due
[d] expense in advance and expense due

19. Explain the adjustment made to the following;
[a] sales   [b] purchases   [c] stock
[d] stationery stock   [e] bad debts

20. Explain how depreciation affects the;
[a] profit and loss account   [b] balance sheet

PPQ 2004
3. (a) *Debtors*   *4000-00*
S. Robinson who owes 1000-00 should be written off.
Provision for bad debts is to created as 5% of the remaining debtors.

From the above information, show ledger accounts, Profit and Loss extract and Balance Sheet extract.

(b) Motor Vehicle = 7000-00

Provision for depreciation 200-00

What is the Motor Vehicle at cost?

Prepare accounts to show the profit and loss extract and an example Balance Sheet of the provision for depreciation.

(An extract is example of how an item is recorded in Profit and loss and Balance Sheet).   [15]

PPQ 1997

6. A company starts in business on 1 January 1994, the financial year end being 31 December. You are to show:

(a) The machinery account.

(b)The provision for depreciation account.

(c) The balance sheet extracts for each of the years 1994, 1995 and 1996.

The machinery bought was:

1994 1 January   1 machine costing 800

1995 1 July   2 machines costing 500 each

1995 1 October   1 machine costing 600

1996 1 April   1 machine costing 200

Depreciation is at the rate of 10 per cent per annum, using the straight line method, machines being depreciated for each proportion of a year.

8. In a new business during the year ended 31 March 1997 the following debts are found to be bad and are written off on the dates shown:

30 June   1996 H. Gwebu   110

31 October 1996 D. Bhembe Ltd.   64

31 December 1996 J. Zwane   12

On 31 March 1997, the schedule of remaining debtors amounting in total to 6,850 is examined, and it is decided to make a provision for doubtful debts of 220.

You are **required** to show:

(a) The bad debts account and the provision for bad debts account.

(b) The charge to the Profit and Loss account.

(c) The relevant extracts from the Balance Sheet as at 31 March 1997.

ANSWERS

14A

7	Drawings	85	
	Purchases		85
	Stock taken for personal use		
13	Bad Debts	630	
	Felicity		630
	Debt written off		
21	Bank	140	
	Bad Debt Recovered		140
	Recovered from Adrian		

14B

Fredric's Balance Sheet as at 31st December 2005

	Cost	Depn	NBV
Capital			29,173
Net Profit			20,319
			49,492
Drawings			1,200
Owners Equity			**48,292**
Fixed Assets	Cost	Depn	NBV
Buildings	39,400	___	39,400
Furniture	4,100	246	3,854
Machinery	2,300	230	2,070
	45,800	476	45,324
Current Assets			
Stock		250	
Debtors	3,310		
Bad Debts	290		
		3,020	
Rent income due		600	
Insurance in Advance		30	
Cash		333	
		4,233	
Current Liabilities			
Bank Overdraft	1,185		
Due for repairs	80		
TCL		1,265	
NCA			2,968
Net Assets			**48,292**

14B

Fredric's Trading, Profit and Loss A/c for the year ended 31st Dec 2005

Sales			48,250
Sales Returns			630
Net Sales			47,620
Opening Stock		410	
Purchases	26,150		
Purchases Returns	574		
Net Purchases		25,576	
Goods available for Sale		25,986	
Closing Stock		250	
Cost of Sales			25,736
Gross Profit			21,884
Rent Income		3,000	
Income due		600	
Rent Earned			3,600
Discount Received			317
Total Income			25,801
Expenses			
Repairs	520		
Amount due	80		
Repairs Expense		600	
Water		330	
wages		2,700	
Insurance	450		
In advance	30		
Insurance Expense		420	
Stationery		220	
Sundry Expenses		160	
Discount Allowed		286	
Bad debts		290	
Depreciation : (246 + 230)		476	
Total Expenses			5,482
Net Profit			20,319

THE PETTY CASHBOOK

15.1 INTRODUCTION

The word **petty** means small. So a **Petty Cashbook** is a subsidiary book where **small payments and small incomes** are recorded before being posted to the ledger. However, provided the receipt or payment is in cash form, the size of the amount doesn't matter; it's all recorded in the petty cashbook. The name petty just comes from the fact that most of the transactions dealing in cash are small. Most of the bigger payments and receipts are in cheque form. Examples of small cash payments include postages, tea, refreshments, stationery, cleaning requirements, and others. The small cash incomes come from counter sales, some debtors, and if its not enough then some is drawn from the bank to meet the small cash payments.

The petty cashbook replaces the cash account. The reason for this is that they needed to know the total amount which had been spent on a particular item. So each of the items of expenditure was allocated a column. And at the period end, they simply found the total for each column.

The cash is stored in a **petty cash box** which is kept on the premises of the business. They don't keep large amounts of cash in it and when it gets beyond the set limit, the excess is deposited with the bank. The petty cashbook is normally under the responsibility of a **Petty Cashier** and we often find ladies in this position.

15.2 PETTY CASHBOOK STRUCTURE

A petty cashbook is illustrated below;

A PETTY CASHBOOK

Dr

Date April	Details	Ref	Total	Bank	Sales	Debtors
1	Balance	b/d	45.0			
1	Bankbook	CB	265.0	265.0		
2	Sales	02	11.0		11.0	
3	Sebastian	03	50.0			50.0
4	Sales	04	10.0		10.0	
6	Simon	05	75.0			75.0
11	Sales	06	15.0		15.0	
20	Belton	07	25.0			25.0
			496.0	265.0	36.0	150.0
			496.0			
	Balance	c/d	151.6			

Cr

Date April	Details	PCV	Total	Post-age	Stat-ionery	Clean-ing	Refresh-ments	Sundry exps	Fo	Other Accounts
2	Stamps		1.50	1.50						
2	Dusters		3.20			3.20				
3	Printer ribbon		19.00		19.00					
4	Sugar		6.20				6.20			
5	Fax		2.30	2.30						
6	Air freshener		5.40			5.40				
7	Paper		23.00		23.00					
8	Tea		2.70				2.70			
9	Stamps		1.20	1.20						
10	Rubber stamp		14.50		14.50					
10	Transport		9.50					9.50		
12	Soap		12.50			12.50				
14	Wages		85.00						NL15	85.00
16	Stamps		1.90	1.90						
17	Cold drinks		10.50				10.50			
19	Envelopes		8.20		8.20					
22	Maintenance		15.00					15.00		
23	Drawings		90.00						GL16	90.00
25	Refreshments		13.00				13.00			
28	Fax		12.50	12.50						
29	Sugar		7.30				7.30			
			344.40	19.40	64.70	21.10	39.70	24.50		175.00
30	Balance	c/d	151.60							
			496.00							

On the **debit side** we record the **cash received** by the petty cashier and each source of income is given a column. We have columns for the date, details, ref, total, and the analysis columns which are allocated to different sources of income. In the **Ref column** we record the number of the source document in case we want to cross check or confirm some information later. The b/d means it was brought down from the previous period. The CB means the corresponding entry is in the cashbook. The others are receipt numbers.

Recording transactions on each of the sides is on a **double entry basis**. The amount is recorded once in the total column and once in the particular analysis column. In our illustration the analysis columns on the debit side are for bank, sales, and debtors. In the bank column we record cash transferred from the bank account. In the sales column we record cash sales. In the debtors column we record cash paid by debtors who were owing. A payment by a debtor appears once in the total column and once in the debtor's column to make it double entry. At the end of the month we find totals for each analysis column including the total column. We get a total of all the cash received and that is in the total column. We then get the total received from each source of income like cash sales and debtor payments. The addition of figures from top to bottom is said to be vertical and it's referred to as **casting**. In order to be sure that every figure in the total column was recorded once in an analysis column, and that there are no addition errors, we get a total of all the totals at the bottom of analysis columns. This is adding horizontally and it's known as **cross casting**. The two totals should be the same and that is the proof of correctness. This is simple on the credit side but the debit is slightly tricky as explained below.

On the **credit side** is where we record **payments** and we have more analysis columns there. We start with a column for the date, then details, the petty cash voucher (PCV) number (section 15.4), the total amount, and the different expense columns. Each kind of expense that is often paid has a special column to itself. We have the **sundry expenses** column where we record small expenses that are not paid often. There is also a multipurpose column where we record the bigger uncommon expenses that have to be posted individually to their accounts in the Ledger. It's called the **"other accounts"** column and is normally the very last column on the credit side. Before this column there is a **folio column** where we record the numbers of the accounts where these amounts are posted as individual figures in the ledger. However, if there are enough columns in the analysis book then each of the entries in this column is allocated a column.

According to our illustration, casting the total column gives us $344.40. To confirm there are no errors we cross cast by adding up the analysis column totals (19.40 + 64.70 + 21.10 + 39.70 + 24.50 + 175.00). When we get the same figure of $344.40 then we are satisfied every figure was recorded twice (in total and analysis column), and that there are no addition errors. Therefore, you should always ensure that the figure from casting is the same as the one from cross casting. If the two totals are not equal then there is an error which should be investigated and corrected. Please **note** that an error of recording an amount in the wrong analysis column is not exposed by a comparison of the vertical and horizontal total.

Casting and cross casting is simple and clear on the credit side but not the debit side, because it has a balance b/d that is recorded only once in the total column. The two totals will never be the same. The casting of totals will always be higher than the cross casting figure, and the difference is the opening balance b/d which is recorded in only the total column. In our illustration casting gives $496, while cross casting gives only $451. The difference between the two is the opening balance b/d of $45.

Counting the cash not used by the end of a period gives us a cash balance but this is not satisfactory because it doesn't consider how much cash was received, and how much was paid out. The correct procedure is **balancing the petty cashbook** where we deduct what was paid out from what was received including the opening balance. During the balancing process we ignore analysis columns and **only use the total columns**. This is the reason why we have a double underline below the analysis column totals and none below the total column totals. We deduct the credit total from the debit total and the difference is recorded on the smaller credit side as a balance c/d. Adding the balance c/d to the credit total gives us a figure which is equivalent to the debit total and they are both double underlined. The balance is b/d for use in the following period. Please note; the credit side is never bigger than the debit side. This means that we can't spend more than what was put in the petty cash box. The worst we can have is where all the cash received was spent, and we have no balance.

The specially printed cash analysis books are normally very large, with many columns to suit the varying needs of different businesses. They are expensive and most students can't afford them. So we improvise by drawing the required columns in the affordable books we have. In order to fit the many columns, we may have to turn our books and use them horizontally.

15.3   SOURCE DOCUMENTS

The source document for petty cash expenses is a **Petty Cash Voucher** which is commonly abbreviated as PCV. It's a document filled in by a Petty Cashier before a cash payment is made. Some of these payments have to be authorised especially if the amounts are large. So after it's filled in, it's taken to an authorised person to check and sign. This voucher is not taken away but remains to prove that cash was paid out, and that it was authorised by the right signature. Below is an illustration of a PCV;

```
┌─────────────────────────────────────────────────────────────┐
│          PETTY CASH VOUCHER                    No.225         │
│  BOLUX MILLING LTD.                                          │
│  P.O.BOX 578, JHB                       Date.....................│
│ ┌──────────────────────────────┬────────────────────────────┐│
│ │          Details             │          Amount            ││
│ ├──────────────────────────────┼────────────────────────────┤│
│ │                              │                            ││
│ │                              │                            ││
│ │                              │                            ││
│ │                              │                            ││
│ │                    Sub-Total │                            ││
│ │                    V.A.T     │                            ││
│ │                    Grand Total│                           ││
│ └──────────────────────────────┴────────────────────────────┘│
│  Charge Account...........................................     │
│  Folio........................                               │
│  Checked & Passed by ......................Sign...............│
│  Received by...............................Sign...............│
└─────────────────────────────────────────────────────────────┘
```

Each voucher has a number that differentiates it from the others. We record this number in the PCV column on the credit side of the petty cashbook. The number is helpful when you need to cross check some figures in the petty cash book against the actual source document. Instead of checking the whole petty cash voucher book, you only look for a particular number.

The PCV shows the detail of expenditure, the account to be charged or column in which to record it, the amount paid, and the date of payment. Both the person authorising the payment and the person receiving the cash have to sign. The folio refers to the account number in the ledger.

The source document for the debit side is the **receipt written** for every cash received. It's indicated on the receipt whether it was a cash sale or a payment by a debtor. If cash came from the bank account it's indicated and we record the cheque number. The top copy receipt is taken by the one who paid, we use the copy left in the receipt book.

15.4   CLASSIFYING TRANSACTIONS

At the place of work, transactions are classified according to what is written as a charge account on the PCV. This tells you which columns to create and in which analysis column to record the amount. However, this is not possible for our exercises at school since we don't use PCVs but just lists of transactions. Therefore, before we make any entries in the petty cashbook, we have to read through all transactions and arrange them **according to the type of expense**. The procedure for classifying expenses is as follows;

i.   Begin by identifying the different groups or kinds of expenses made and write them on a piece of paper.

ii.   Classify all transactions one by one, noting the group in which each one of them falls, and indicating on the paper how many transactions each group of expense has.

iii.   Allocate a column to each group of expense that has more than one transaction, and the names of these groups are written as headings for the analysis columns.

iv.   Those groups of expenses that have only one transaction and are small in amount do not need to be allocated a column, they are all recorded in the **sundry expenses column**. Their number is not big enough for each category to be allocated a column on their own.

v.   Allocate the last column to the bigger expenses that appear only once and have to be recorded in the **multi-purpose column** referred to as **"other accounts"** column.

Transactions for the debit side are easier since there are not many different sources of income. We use information recorded on the receipt, which indicates whether it should be recorded in the cash sales, debtors, or bank transfer column.

Using the following transactions, classify and record them in a petty cashbook.
2005 April 1st Cash balance brought down $45.00
1st   Cashed a cheque of $265 for petty expenses
2nd   Bought stamps for $1.50
2nd   Paid for cleaning dusters for $3.20
2nd   Sold goods for cash $11.00
3rd   Purchased printer ribbon for $19.00
3rd   A debtor, Sebastian paid $50.00
4th   Bought 2kgs of sugar at $6.20
4th   Received $10.00 from cash sales
5th   Sent a fax at a cost of $2.30
6th   Purchased air freshener at $5.40

6th   Simon a debtor paid $75.00
7th   Paid $23.00 for a ream of paper
8th   Bought 1 packet of Tea at $2.70
9th   Purchased stamps for $1.20
10th   Cost of new rubber stamp was paid, $14.50
10th   Gave bus fare to office messenger, $9.50
11th   Made cash sales for $15.00
12th   Purchased liquid soap at $12.50
14th   Paid wages to temporary worker, $85.00
16th   Paid for stamps at $1.90
17th   Bought some cold drinks for visitors for $10.50
19th   Paid for two packets of envelops at $8.20
20th   A debtor, Belton paid $25.00
22nd   Paid $15 for maintenance of the door lock.
23rd   The owner took $90 for personal use
25th   Bought some refreshments for $13.00
28th   Sent a fax at a cost of $12.50
29th   Purchased sugar at a cost of $7.30

The above transactions can be arranged in expense groups as follows;

Expense type	frequency	total frequency
Postages	IIIII	5
Stationery	IIII	4
Cleaning	III	3
Refreshments	IIIII	5
Maintenance	I	1
Wages	I	1
Drawings	I	1
Transport	I	1

From this classification process, expenses with more than one transaction are each allocated a column and they are; postages, stationery, cleaning, and refreshments. Among the expenses that have only one transaction we identify those with large amounts. Those are to be posted to their individual accounts in the ledger and they are wages $85 and drawings$90. So they are recorded in the "other accounts" column. However, if there is no shortage of columns, each of the entries in this column is allocated its own column. The other types of expenses with only one transaction and yet the amounts are small are recorded in the sundry expenses column. This column is reserved for the **small uncommon expenses**.

There should be only 3 analysis columns on the debit side; one for Bank, Debtors, and cash sales.
The petty cashbook prepared should be the same as the one illustrated above. **Please confirm.**

EX 15A. *The following information relates to Sabs Investments for November 2006. He was given a cash float of $120 on the 1st of the month. You are required to prepare and balance their petty cashbook using the postages, stationery, cleaning and other accounts columns.*

4th   Stamps were bought for $4.70
7th   Purchased pens for office use at $7.45
9th   Bought omo micro at $5.25
10th   Some petrol was bought at $25.00
15th   Paid for cleaning dusters at $2.70
17th   Sent a fax to Johannesburg at $5.50
20th   Drew $45.00 from the petty cash box for personal use.
22nd   Paper carbons were bought at $7.80
23rd   A Telegram was sent at a cost of $3.20
26th   Purchased pencils for office work at $2.10

EX 15B. *From the following information relating to September 2002, you are required to prepare and balance a petty cashbook for Thomas. Use the postages, stationery, sundry expenses and other accounts columns.*

1st   He was given a cheque of $200 for his cash float
4th   He sent a registered letter which cost $8.10
7th   He bought a ream of paper at $24.50
11th   Paid $10.90 for omo micro
13th   Filled the business car with petrol for $19.50
17th   Purchased pens for office use at $4.75
18th   Bought refreshments while on a trip for $9.50
20th   Sent a telegram which cost $4.30
23rd   Used $65.00 f for personal expenses
26th   Paid for stamps at $2.10
28th   Bought a packet of envelops at $5.50
29th   Purchased some pencils for office use at $2.40

15.5   POSTING THE PETTY CASHBOOK

The petty cashbook is a subsidiary book and a section of the ledger. It reduces the detail of transactions to only totals that we post to the ledger. Being a section of the ledger, it accommodates one of the entries. Therefore, what we post to the ledger is the second entry to complete double entry. What may be different is that the total figure posted, has several smaller corresponding entries.

The only figures we post are the totals in the analysis columns. From the debit side the $150 is credited to the debtors control account, the $36 to the sales account, and the $265 to the Bankbook. However, because we need to have

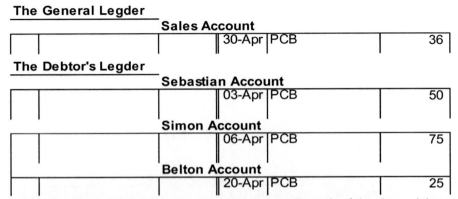

The General Legder
Sales Account

				30-Apr	PCB		36

The Debtor's Legder
Sebastian Account

				03-Apr	PCB		50

Simon Account

				06-Apr	PCB		75

Belton Account

				20-Apr	PCB		25

an update of what the debtors are owing, we credit each of the three debtors who paid, with the respective amounts of $50, $75, and $25. Therefore, debtor payments are posted individually as illustrated below;

The narration for each of these postings is petty cashbook which it abbreviated by PCB. That is where their corresponding entries are located.

From the credit side we post the totals at the bottom of each analysis column **except** the other "other Accounts" column. They are posted to the debit side of the account written as heading for the column. We debit $19.40 to the postages account, $64.70 to the stationery account, $21.10 to the cleaning account, $39.70 to the refreshments account, and $24.50 to the sundry expenses account. We don't post the total of the "other accounts" column, each of the figures in the column is posted individually to its respective account. In our illustration on the following page, the $85 is posted to wages account and the $90 is posted to the drawings account.

We record folio numbers below the column totals and this is after they have been posted and their account numbers are identified. For the figures that are posted individually, their folio numbers are recorded in the **folio column** between the last analysis column and the "other accounts" column. The folio number NL6 below the postages column means that the postages account is found in the nominal ledger and its account number 6. GL means general ledger. The credit side of the petty cashbook on page 164 is posted to the ledger as follows;

The Nominal Ledger

Postages Account [6]

30-Apr	Petty cash	19.40	

Stationery Account [10]

30-Apr	Petty cash	64.70	

Cleaning Account [11]

30-Apr	Petty cash	21.10	

Refreshments Account [14]

30-Apr	Petty cash	39.70	

Sundry Expenses Account [22]

30-Apr	Petty cash	24.50	

Wages Account [15]

30-Apr	Petty cash	85.00	

The General Ledger

Drawings Account [16]

30-Apr	Petty cash	90.00	

EX 15C. Using the information provided in exercise 15A and the petty cashbook prepared, you are required to post to the ledger.

EX 15D. You are required to post the petty cashbook prepared in exercise 15B to the ledger.

15.6   THE IMPREST SYSTEM

The imprest system is where a petty cashier is given cash and the amount spent is **replaced** at every beginning of the period. Some businesses replace it every week, while others replace it every fortnight or monthly. The maximum amount the petty cashier should have at every beginning of the period is what we refer to as the **imprest amount, or cash float.** The Petty Cashier is authorised to spend it during the period and a total of what was spent is **replaced** to restore them back to the imprest amount. The amount is replaced just before, or at the start of the following period.

However, before the Accountant or Treasurer replaces the amount spent, the Petty Cashier has to **account for it** – explain and show how it was spent. For example, if the imprest amount is $100 and they spent $61.50 during the period, it leaves a balance of only $38.50. So in order to restore them to the imprest amount of $100, they replace the $61.50 that is equal to what was spent.

It's possible to **check if there is no money missing** in the petty cash box by totalling the amounts on the petty cash vouchers, and adding to the cash available. The total should be equal to the imprest amount. If the total does not come to the imprest amount then there is either cash missing, or a petty cash voucher missing.

The amount required to restore the imprest is equal to the amount spent. However, if there was some income received then the amount required to restore the imprest is equal to the amount spent, less the income received.

Multiple Choice & Short Answer Questions

1. Which of the following is recorded in the petty cashbook?
A. Debtor pays by cheque   B. Purchase of cold drinks for the office
C. Cheque sent to the creditor   D. Purchase of furniture on credit

2. One of the following is not recorded in the petty cashbook?
A. Postages   B. Assets
C. Stationery   D. Cleaning expenses

3. The petty cashbook replaces the
A. Cash account   B. Bank account
C. Postages   D. Cashbook

4. The source document for expenses recorded in the petty cashbook is
A. Deposit slip   B. Petty cash voucher
C. Cheque   D. Receipt

5. Another name for the imprest amount is
A. Imprest system   B. Cash float
C. Petty cash   D. Cash balance

6. The system of replacing the cashier's amount spent the previous period is known as
A. Imprest system   B. Cash float
C. Petty cash   D. Cash balance

7. The bigger expenses which appear only once are recorded in the
A. First column   B. Total column
C. Other accounts column   D. Folio column

8. The amount required to restore the cash float is equal to
A. Cash float   B. Cash received
C. Cash available   D. Cash spent

9. From the credit side of the petty cashbook we post
A. Individual entries   B. Column totals
C. The total column   D. The total of totals

10. Which column total is not posted to the ledger?
A. Creditor's total   B. Debtor's total
C. Other accounts   D. Sundry expenses

11. The subsidiary book where we record small cash payments is the
A. Cashbook   B. Petty cashbook
C. Bank account   D. None of these

12. If a petty cash box contains $120 at a particular date and the petty cash vouchers at that date total $180, then the petty cash imprest amount should be:
A. 120   B. 180   C. 300   D. 60

13. To restore the petty cash imprest in question 12 above to it's original level, the cashier should ask for

A.   120   B. 180   C. 300   D. 60

14. All the descriptions below suit   the expenses recorded   in the   "other amounts" column except

A. a large amount   B   uncommon expense

C. those posted individually   D   a small amount

15. Explain the operation of the imprest system.

16. How do you record and balance the petty cashbook?

17. Explain the process of posting the petty cashbook to the ledger.

PPQ 2002

5. The following information relates to Sabelo Gifted's Investments for November. He was given a cash float of 120- 00 at the beginning of the month.

Nov-04 Stamps were purchased for	4.70
Nov-07 Purchased pens	7.45
Nov-09 Bought Omo Micro	5.25
Nov-10 Bought petrol	25.00
Nov-15 Paid for cleaning dusters	2.70
Nov-17 Sent a letter to Simunye	5.50
Nov-20 Drew 45.00 from the Petty Cashbook for personal use	
Nov-22 Paper carbons were bought	7.80
Nov-23 A telegram was sent at	3.20
Nov-26 Purcahsed pencils for office work at	2.10

You are required to prepare and balance his Petty Cash Book using amongst others the following columns; postage, stationary, ledger and cleaning.

PPQ 2000

5. The Mzimnene Grocery Store controls its petty cash by means of a monthly imprest of R200. **Write up** the petty cash book using not more than four analysis columns.

Nov.01 Bought stationery	2.00
5 Paid cleaner	10.00
8 Bought stamps	2.00
12 Window cleaner	4.00
15 Bought stamps	1.00
28 Bought pens, pencil ink	10.00
30 Paid for office cleaning	10.00

PPQ 1999

4. *On 1st January R100 cash was handed to the petty cashier to pay petty cash expenses for the month, which were as follows:*

March-01	Postage stamps	25.00
3	Car wash	2.50
4	Bus fare	1.30
5	Shorthand note books	5.20
6	Postage stamps	10.00
8	Fare to Lavumisa	12.50
9	Cleaning	5.00
11	Pencils	1.50
14	Exam pads	2.50
16	Envelopes	2.00
18	Stationery	8.00
31	Tea and coffee	7.00

Rule *a petty cash book in analysis form, with four analysis columns, headed postages and telephone, travelling expenses, stationery, and sundry expenses. Enter the foregoing items and close the books as on 31 January, showing clearly the balance of cash in hand.*

PPQ 1996

5a. i. *What is the use of the Petty Cashbook?*
ii. *What is the Imprest System?*

b. *Enter the following in the petty cash book using separate columns for; Postage and telegrams; Carriage; stationery. Balance the Cash Book as at 10th January 1996*

January 4	balance in hand	15.00	
January 4	paid postage stamps		1.50
January 5	paid for stationery	3.50	
January 5	paid for carriage	0.85	
January 6	paid for stamps		1.25
January 8	paid for stationery	1.50	

How much will the petty cashier receive to cover petty cash expenditure for the days after 10th January?

PPQ 1994

5. (a) Explain briefly the working of the Imprest Petty Cash System.
(5]

(b) Give as an illustration a ruling (with three analysis columns),
and enter therein the following items:

Jan-01	Balance in hand (float)	20.00
5	Paid for postage stamps	1.50
7	Paid for telegrams	0.53
10	Paid for office tea, etc.	0.95
14	Paid for sundry cash purchases of goods for resale	8.37
20	Paid for stationary	1.12
23	Paid for postage	0.20
23	Paid for subscription to trade periodical	2.10
31	Received reimbursement for the month's expenditure to restore the float	

[10]

PPQ 1990

6. On 1 March E100 cash was handed to the Petty Cashier to pay
Petty cash expenses for the month, which were as follows;

March 1	Postage stamps	20.00
3	Carriage	2.30
4	Bus fare	0.30
5	Short hand note books	5.20
6	Postage stamps	10.00
8	Fare to Mbabane	12.55
9	Sundry Trade Expenses	5.14
11	Pencils	1.40
14	Newspaper	0.50
16	Envelopes	2.41
18	Stationery	8.70
31	Carriage	7.20

Rule a petty Cash book in analysis form, with five analysis columns,
headed Postages and Telephone, Carriages, traveling expenses,
stationery and sundry trade expenses respectively. Enter the
foregoing items and close the books as on 31 March, showing
clearly the balance of cash in hand.

CHAPTER 16

BANK RECONCILIATION

This chapter covers: page

16.1   Introduction

Bank Reconciliation is the process of finding the causes of difference between the bank account balance and bank statement balance. Both the bank account and bank statement are a record of transactions between a particular business and the bank. The bank account is maintained in the business by its staff, while the bank statement is prepared by banking staff. The bank sends a copy of the statement to the business at every month end. The balance on the statement is most often different from what is on the account.

16.2   A Bank Statement

A bank statement shows transactions between the business and the bank. It shows deposits, withdrawals, bank charges, dishonoured cheques, and others. It's like any other **vertical account** where a balance is calculated after each entry. It has columns as illustrated below.

RACHEL'S BANK STATEMENT FOR PERIOD ENDING 31.05.2000					
Date	Details	Debit	Credit	Balance	
May-1	Balance b/d			285	
3	deposit		850	1,135	
6	cheque no.719	430		705	
9	cheque book	5		700	
10	deposit		200	900	
14	deposit		370	1,270	
16	deposit		260	1,530	
17	commission	10		1,520	
18	cheque no. 720	1,100		420	
20	deposit		225	645	
23	deposit		315	960	
26	deposit		290	1,250	
29	cheque no. 721	90		1,160	
30	ledger fee	35		1,125	
31	cheque no 722	1,400		(275)	OD

In the **debit column** they record amounts drawn from the bank. The assumption is that they **received** the cash although some of it goes straight to creditors, and expenses paid by cheque. This is based on the double entry principle of debiting the receiver.

In the **credit column** they record the cash and cheques deposited to the account. This is based on the principle of crediting the account holder who is the giver. When a cheque is dishonoured, an entry in the credit column is reversed by recording it in the debit column.

A balance is calculated after each entry and it's recorded in the **balance column.** Every entry in the debit column reduces the balance, while an entry in the credit column (deposits) increases the balance on the account. The cash on the account is the last balance at the bottom. It's indicated by a figure above zero. If the statement has a balance with **OD** written next to it then it has been **over drawn**. This means the amount drawn in excess of the balance was borrowed from the bank, and it's a negative balance. A negative (overdrawn) balance is indicated by a negative sign or putting it in brackets. On the statement above, the closing balance is an overdrawn balance of £275 which is indicated by **OD** next to it.

16.3   Bank Account And Statement Entries
Entries made on a bank account and bank statement are **opposite** to each other, although they both follow the double entry principle. When the business deposits cash or cheque, the bank account is debited since bank is the receiver. When the bank receives the cash or cheque, it credits the statement since the business is the giver, and debits its bank account (the receiver). So for the same transaction, the **bank account is debited** while the **bank statement is credited**, they are opposite to each other.

When the business draws cash, pays by cheque, or pays bank charges, the bank account is credited since it's the giver. When that money leaves, the bank debits the business' statement, and credits its bank account. So for the same transaction, the **bank statement is debited** while the **bank account is credited.**

16.4   Bank Account And Bank Statement Differences
The balance on a bank account is often not the same as the balance on a bank statement. The reason is that they each contain transactions which are not yet on the other. Therefore, whenever a statement is received, a responsible person is supposed to check it against the bank account and find reasons for the difference in balances.   There are several causes of differences which include; unpresented cheques, cheques not credited, direct

credits, standing orders, direct debits, bank charges, dishonoured cheques, and others. Below is an explanation of the different causes and how the difference can be eliminated.

Unpresented Cheques (UPC)

These are cheques used for payment but are not yet presented to the bank by the statement date. Cheques only appear on the statement after they have been presented to the bank. As soon as the cheque is written, the bank account is credited and yet the one paid takes their time to present it. So it appears on the bank account and its balance is reduced, but doesn't appear on the bank statement and it has a higher balance. Since the money is not yet removed from the bank, the balance on the bank account is raised **by adding back unpresented cheques.** This is done during the reconciliation process.

Cheques Not Credited (CNC)

These are cheques received from debtors /buyers but they don't appear on the bank statement. They only appear on the statement after they are cleared. **Clearing** is a process where the bank transfers money from the drawer's account to its client's account. It may take a few days depending on the efficiency of the banking system.

The bank account is debited soon after taking cheques to the bank and this raises its balance, but the statement is not yet credited and it has a lower balance. Since the money is not yet on the account, this difference is eliminated **by deducting these cheques** from the bank account balance. This is done during the reconciliation process.

Direct Credit (DC)

A Direct credit is money received by the bank on behalf of the business and credits or **deposits** it to the account. The business may not be aware of this money until it receives the statement. This means the statement has the entry and has a higher balance, while the bank account doesn't and has a lower balance. This difference is eliminated **by updating and debiting the bank account,** which increases its balance.

Standing Order (SO)

A standing order is an instruction **from the account holder** to the bank, to make regular payments of a fixed amount, for a particular period of time. As the bank makes the payment, it debits the statement and this reduces the balance. However, the bank account is not credited due to forgetfulness or some other reason and it has a higher balance. This difference is eliminated **by updating and crediting the bank account,** which reduces its balance.

Direct Debit (DD)

This is an instruction **authorised by the account holder but initiated by their supplier**, asking the bank to pay them. Money is transferred directly from the holder's account to the suppliers account. The aim of this service is to relieve the account holder from the need to write cheques every month. So the supplier who is keen about getting paid is the one who follows up the bank. The difference between this service and standing order is that this one is initiated by the creditor-supplier. Secondly, the amount changes every month and that is why the supplier, who knows the new invoice value, is the one who communicates to the bank. Examples are telephone and electricity bills which change every month.

	Differences between	
	Standing Order and	**Direct Debit**
1.	Initiated by account holder	Initiated by creditor
2.	Amount is same every month	Amount is different every month
3.	Both are authorised by the acccount holder	

Just like a standing order, a direct debit causes a difference that is eliminated **by updating and crediting the bank account.**

Bank Charges (BC)

This is money charged by a bank for the services it provides. This money is not paid physically by account holders but **deducted** by bank from the account. The business only gets this information from the statement. So the bank debits the statement and reduces the balance. The bank account is not credited and it has a higher balance. This difference is eliminated **by updating and crediting** the bank account.

Dishonoured Cheques (RD)

A Dishonoured Cheque is one against which the bank refuses to pay. This means the money on the cheque wasn't credited to the statement.

For learning purposes, the bank credits the statement on receipt of a cheque. When it's dishonoured the bank reverses the cheque by debiting the statement. The business may only get this information from the statement at month end. So the bank statement is already debited and has a lower balance than the bank account which is not yet credited. This difference is eliminated **by updating and crediting the bank account** with dishonoured cheques.

16.5   Bank Reconciliation Process

Bank Reconciliation is a process which identifies the causes of difference and enables the account and statement balances to **agree.** It effectively updates the bank account and adjusts its balance. It is a three step process that includes;

identifying the causes of difference; updating the bank account; and adjusting the bank account balance.

The causes of difference are identified through a checking process.

♦   The first step is to **compare** the figures on the **debit side of a bank account** with those in the **credit column on the statement**. Figures appearing on both are ticked with a pencil and this leaves some without ticks. Those without ticks are some of the causes of difference since they appear on only the account or statement.

♦   The figures on the **credit side of bank account** are **compared** with those in the **debit column** on the statement. The ones that appear on both are ticked. Those without ticks are identified as some of the causes of difference.

Below is an illustration of a compared bank account and statement.

Mable's Bank account for the month ended 30th April 2005

1	Balance	b/d	690	1	Rent paid	500 ✔
2	Sales		367 ✔	4	Hilda	285 ✔
6	Allan		180 ✔	8	Purchases	400 ✔
10	Sales		498	13	Andrew	270
16	Martha		324 ✔	23	Repairs	193
19	Commission earned		130 ✔	26	Wages	380 ✔
27	James		470	28	Abraham	350
				29	Balance c/d	281
			2,659			2,659
1	Balance b/d		281			

Mable's Bank Statement as at 30th April 2005

Date	Details	Debit	Credit	Balance
1	Balance b/d			690
1	Cheque no. 215	500 ✔		190
2	Deposit		367 ✔	557
4	Cheque no. 216	285 ✔		272
6	Deposit		180 ✔	452
8	Cheque no. 217	400 ✔		52
16	Deposit		324 ✔	376
17	DD--Violet		450	826
19	Deposit		130 ✔	956
25	DD--Edward		305	1,261
26	Cheque no. 220	380 ✔		881
29	SO--water	125		756

29	SO--insurance	49	707	
29	Salim-- **R/D**	324	383	

16.6   Updating The Bank Account

After ticking off, the next step is to update the bank account with those **figures on the bank statement that do not have ticks**. So we compile a fresh bank account titled **"updated bank account"**.

♦ We start with a balance or overdraft brought down at the end of the period. Enter the figures without ticks in the **credit column** of the statement, to the **debit side** of the bank account.

♦ Record the figures without ticks in the **debit column** on the statement, to the **credit side** of the bank account.

♦ Work out the **new balance** on the bank account.

Below is an updated bank account basing on illustrations above;

Mable's Updated Bank Account

30	Balance b/d	281	29	DD - Water	125
17	DC - Violet	450	29	DD - Insurance	49
25	DC - Edward	305	29	Salim R/D	324
				Balance c/d	538
		1,036			1,036
	Balance b/d	538			

EX 16A. Miriam's Bank Account for month ended 30th April 2001

1	Balance b/d	318	2	Stationery	95
3	Sales	290	5	Purchases	250
7	Luke	460	13	Hudson	418
19	Rent received	500	22	Electricity	130
24	Martin	362	25	Motor expenses	55
			28	Maria	620
			30	Balance c/d	362
		1,930			1,930
1	Balance b/d	362			

Miriam's Bank Statement as at 30th April 2001

Date	Details	Debit	Credit	Balance
1	Balance b/d			318
2	Cheque No. 949	95		223
3	Deposit		290	513
4	SO-insurance	83		430
5	Cheque No. 950	250		180
7	Deposit		460	640
13	Cheque No. 951	418		222
19	Deposit		500	722
22	Cheque No. 952	130		592
25	Cheque No. 953	55		537
26	DD-- Mbongeni		235	772

Compile an updated bank account, starting with a balance b/d.

16.7   Bank Reconciliation Statement

This is a statement where we adjust the updated bank account balance to agree with the bank statement balance. It's **the final step** in the reconciliation process and it **reverses entries** made on the bank account that are not yet on the statement.

We start with a balance or overdraft as per updated bank account

We add unpresented cheques and deduct cheques not credited in order to arrive at the same balance or overdraft on the bank statement.

+ UPC – CNC

This is based on the following understanding;

Unpresented cheques: They were credited in the cashbook but they don't yet affect the balance on the account in the bank. In order to raise the cashbook balance to the same level as bank statement, they have to be **added back.**

Cheques not Credited: They were debited in the cashbook but they don't yet affect the balance on the account in the bank. In order to reduce the cashbook balance to the same level as bank statement, they have to be **deducted.**

Below is an illustration of a reconciliation statement. It's reconciling the bank statement and updated bank account on pages 181 and 182.

Bank Reconciliation Statement		
Balance per Updated Bank Account		538
add Unpresented Cheques :	270	
	193	
	+ 350	
		+ 813
		1,351
less Cheques not Credited :	498	
	+ 470	
		- 968
Balance per Bank Statement		383

What we record on the **balance sheet** is the actual amount on the account and that is the balance on the bank statement.

EX 16B. Using the bank account and bank statement provided in exercise 16A, write the bank reconciliation statement starting with a balance per bank account.

EX 14C. **Nadine's Bank account for the month ended 30th September 2004**

1	Balance	b/d	282	4	Purchases		520
2	Sales		335	10	Stationery		110
7	Susie		508	18	Advertising		90
15	Rent received		450	21	Patrick		310
20	Sales		290	24	Wages		850
27	Brian		170	29	Daniel		345
30	Overdraft	c/d	190				
			2,225				2,225
				1	Overdraft	b/d	190

Nadine's Bank Statement as at 30th September 2004

Date	Details	Debit	Credit	Balance
1	Balance b/d			282
2	Deposit		335	617
4	Cheque no. 736	520		97
7	Deposit		508	605
10	Cheque no. 737	110		495
23	**DD-** Thembi		145	640
24	Cheque no. 740	850		210 **OD**
27	Deposit		170	40 **OD**
28	**SO--**motor expenses	150		190 **OD**
29	Cheque no. 741	345		535 **OD**
30	Bank charges	43		578 **OD**

You are **required** to write an updated bank account,
and the bank reconciliation statement.

16.10   The Importance Of Bank Reconciliation

The reconciliation process achieves the following;

1. Direct Credits: We are able to identity the cash received by the bank on behalf of the business. When the bank account is updated, its balance goes up.

2. Direct Debits: We are able to identity payments made by the bank on behalf of the business. When the bank account is updated, its balance goes down.

3.   Errors: Through the reconciliation process, we are able to identify and correct errors made by either the accounting staff in charge of the cashbook, or the banking staff.

4. Fraud: Through the reconciliation process, we may identify fraud done on the account.

5.   Updating: The overriding purpose of bank reconciliation is to update the bank account in the cashbook. We get to know the actual transactions on the account in the bank, and get the actual balance for use on the balance sheet.

MULTIPLE CHOICE & SHORT ANSWER QUESTIONS

1.   A bank statement shows
A. Statement of affairs   B. Profits in the bank
C. Transactions between the business and the bank
D. The account for the bank

2. On the bank statement, cash deposited is recorded in the
A. Details column   B. Debit column
C. Credit column   D. Balance column

3. The balance column on the bank statement shows the ....
after every transaction.
A. Cash deposited   B. Cash on the account
C. Cash withdrawn   D. Bank charges

4. Unpresented cheques are
A. Already paid   B. Deposited
C. Dishonoured   D. Not yet cashed

5.   When a cheque is presented for cashing to the bank the balance on the account
A. Reduces   B. Increases
C. Grows   D. Does not change

6. When a cheque is cleared the balance on the account
A. Reduces   B. Increases
C. Goes down   D. Does not change

7. Information about a direct deposit gets to the account holder through a
A. Cash book   B. Bank statement
C. Direct debit   D. Standing order

8. The instruction to make uniform regular payments on behalf of the account holder is a
A. Direct deposit   B. Cleared cheque
C. Standing order   D. Direct debit

9. If the bank refuses to pay cash against a cheque then it's said to be
A. Cleared   B. Presented   C. Unpresented   D. Dishonoured

10. The process of finding the cause of difference between the bank account and bank statement is
A. Cash reconciliation   B. statement of affairs
C. Bank reconciliation   D. Control reconciliation

11. To update the bank account   we get information from the
A. Bank account   B. Cash account
C. Bank statement   D. Petty cash account

12. When updating the bank account, bank charges are
A. Debited to the bank account B. Credited to the bank account
C. Debited to bank statement   D. Credited to bank statement

13. During the reconciliation process direct deposits are
A. Debited to the bank account   B. Credited to the bank account
C. Debited to bank statement   D. Credited to bank statement
14. Explain the causes of differences between the bank account and bank statement balances?

14D	Ivan's Bank Account for the month ended 29th February 2000			
1	Balance b/d	690	1	Rent paid	500
2	Sales	367	4	Hilary	285
6	Sandra	180	8	Purchases	400
10	Sales	498	13	Becky	270
16	Veronica	324	23	Repairs	193
19	Commission earned	130	26	Wages	380
27	Sophia	470	28	Geoffrey	350
			29	Balance c/d	281
		2,659			2,659
1	Balance b/d	281			

Ivan's Bank Statement as at 29th February 2000

Date	Details	Debit	Credit	Balance
1	Balance b/d			690
1	Cheque no. 215	500		190
2	Deposit		367	557
4	Cheque no. 216	285		272
6	Deposit		180	452
8	Cheque no. 217	400		52
16	Deposit		324	376
17	DD--Violet		450	826
19	Deposit		130	956
25	DD--Edward		305	1,261
26	Cheque no. 220	380		881
29	SO--water	125		756
29	SO--Insurance	49		707
29	Veronica-- **R/D**	324		383

PPQ 2005
5. *Below are extracts from the cash (bank column only) and the bank statement of a trader, for the month of January 2001.*

2001 January			CashBook		
Dr		**E**	**Cr**		**E**
			2	Sibiya	100
1	Balance	500	3	Thwala	300
6	Simelane	60	24	Wages	60
10	Bhembe	200	25	Khumalo	40
17	Gule	50	29	Dvuba	150
28	Dlamini	200	29	Simelane	60
			31	Balance c/d	300
		1010			1010

Bank Statement

2001 January		Dr	Cr	Balance	
1	Balance			650	
2	F. Shongwe		50	700	
2	Sibiya	100		600	
3	Mamba	200		400	
5	Thwala	300		100	
20	Bhembe		200	300	
21	Bank charges	5		295	
23	Interest earned		155	450	
24	Wages	60		390	
31	Insurance Standing order	110		280	(15)

You are **required** to prepare a reconciliation statement.

PPQ 2004

2. The balance as per Cash book for month of June 2001 was 864-00 debit. However, there were cheques written to pay our Creditors but they had still not taken the cheques to the bank for payment. The Creditors were Robert Khumalo whom we owed 395, Bobert Dlamini 196 and Joyce Maseko 300. When we checked our bank statement we also discovered the cheques which we took to the bank had not been indicated as credit in our bank account. These were cheques received from Sandziso Zwane for 236, Sabelo Maziya 300 and Rejoice Nyawo 600.

From the above information, you are **required** to prepare a bank reconciliation statement showing clearly the balance as per Bank Statement for the month of June 30 2001.

[15]

PPQ 2003

4. Explain each of the following in relation to the bank reconciliation process
(i) Unpresented cheques   [3]
(ii) Cheques not yet cleared   [3]
(iii) Direct deposits   [3]
(iv) Standing orders   [3]
(v) Debtors dishonoured cheques   [3]

PPQ 2002

1. A firm's Cash book (Bank column only) for the month of November 1982 was as follows:

Nov-01	Balance b/d	570	Nov-01	B Zwane	120
Nov-09	S. Donates	60	Nov-12	G. Maziya	280
Nov-12	Cash Sales	205	Nov-24	P. Dlamini	65
Nov-18	W. Papuna	100	Nov-31	Balance c/d	640
Nov-30	P. Dlomo	170			
		1,105			1,105

In early December the following bank statement was received from the bank

	Details	Dr	Cr	Balance
Nov-01	Balance b/f			570
6	Cheque paid	120		450
9	Cheque		60	510
12	Cash		205	715
16	Standing Order-Insurance	80		635
18	Cheque		100	735
25	Credit tranfer		130	865
28	Cheque	65		800
31	Bank charges	12		788

You are required to:
(a) Bring the Cash book up to date.
(b) Prepare a statement to reconcile the difference between the Cash book balance and the bank statement on 31 Nov 1982.

[15]

Answers

14A

Miriam's Updated Bank Account

	Balance b/d	362	4	SO - Insurance	83
26	DD - Mbongeni	235		Balance c/d	514
		597			597
	Balance b/d	514			

14B
Bank Reconciliation Statement

Balance per Cashbook	514
Unpresented Cheque	620
	1,134
Cheque not credited	362
Balance per Bank Statement	772

CHAPTER 17

PARTNERSHIPS

This chapter covers:

17.1 Introduction

A partnership is a business organisation owned by a minimum of two and maximum of 20 partners. The owners of this business are the partners who contribute capital. Issues are discussed among themselves before decisions are made. Partnerships are common in trade and among professionals like Lawyers, Accountants, Doctors, and others.

The contribution of capital, interest on capital, partner's salaries, sharing of profits and the general running of the business is written down in an agreement called a **partnership deed**. It states the terms and conditions of their business, and is submitted to the Registrar of Companies before the partnership is allowed to start operating.

17. 2 Partnership Advantages And Disadvantages

Advantages

1. They are able to raise a **larger amount of capital** since its more than one person contributing.

2. The **responsibilities** of the business are **shared** among the different partners like selling stock, buying stock and others.

3. Business continues even if one partner dies or leaves the business. The other partners continue running it.

4. Losses are shared among the partners and each one takes a small portion of the total loss.

5. Ideas and decisions are first discussed and this leads to **less mistakes.**

Disadvantages

1. The sharing of a **small profit** may leave some partners **dissatisfied**.

2. Discussions before a decision may lead to **arguments** that may cause conflict and the breaking up of business.

3. Any **mistake** by one partner is **suffered by all** the partners since they act on behalf of the others.

17. 3   Partnership Accounts

The Bookkeeping or Accounts looked at from the beginning of this book refers to a sole trader. **A sole trader** is an individual who contributes capital and owns a business alone. They enjoy all profits and bear all the losses alone. The **accounting records** for a partnership are **very similar** to those of a sole trader. They write all subsidiary books, post to the ledger, extract a trial balance, make adjustments, prepare a trading, and profit and loss account, and balance sheet. These are standard accounts for any business. Differences arise when it comes to opening statements, the appropriation account, capital accounts, current accounts, and the balance sheet. Those are the areas where a partnership is different from a sole trader, and that is the emphasis of this chapter.

17. 4   Opening Statements

An opening statement is written before we start writing double entry accounting. In the case of a partnership, an opening statement is written for each partner and it should balance before they are merged to get the overall opening statement.

Below is an illustration of Diana and Doris' opening statements;

Diana		
Furniture	5,400	
Bank	3,500	
Cash	750	
Capital		9,650
Being opening balances for Diana	9,650	9,650

Doris		
Stock	4,800	
Bank	2,550	
Cash	1,100	
Capital		8,450
	8,450	8,450
Being opening balances for Doris		

These two are merged by adding the various items to get the opening
statement for the partnership as illustrated below;

Furniture	5,400	
Stock	4,800	
Bank (3500 + 2550)	6,050	
Cash (750 + 1100)	1,850	
Capital (9650 + 8450)		18,100
	18,100	18,100
Being opening balances for the Partnership		

EXERCISE 17A.
*You are required to prepare opening statements for the following
partners and find their capital contribution.*
Deborah *brought in; cash $500, bank $1,600, furniture $3,500 and
stock $2,700.*
Cynthia *brought in; bank $900, equipment $4,300 and stock $3,100.
You should also compile a* **combined opening statement.**

17.5   Sharing Net Profit
A sole trader doesn't share net profit with any body. In a partnership, the net
profit is shared among the partners basing on the partnership deed. Net profit
is divided up on the basis of; interest on capital, partner's salaries, and
residual net profit.

Interest on Capital: This is a reward given to partners in return for the risk of
contributing capital to the business. It's the price paid by the business for
using the partner's capital. It's normally expressed as a **percentage** and the
bigger the amount invested, the bigger the amount they get as interest. The
rate of interest may not be much different from what they would earn if they
invested it elsewhere. The percentage used is agreed earlier in the
partnership deed.

Salary: This is a reward paid to a partner in return for their time or service
provided to the business. The more time or service provided, the higher the
salary. Partners who don't provide it don't earn a salary. Please note that
according to the **law**, salaries paid to the owners are not a business expense.
This is the reason why these salaries are not on the income statement but on
the appropriation account.

Residual Net Profit (RNP): This is what remains after deducting partner
salaries and interest on capital from profit. It's shared among the partners
basing on their **profit sharing ratio**. They use a ratio and not an amount since
they are not sure how much profit or loss the business will make.

A ratio is similar to a percentage and it says that whatever amount of residual profit, you get 33.33 %. This implies that out of every $100 residual profit, you get $33.33. In terms of ratios, 33.33% is equivalent to 1:2. The total number of portions is 1+2 = 3. 1 portion is equal to 33.33% and the two portions are equal to 66.67%. Profit sharing ratios are influenced by the amount of capital invested, the services provided to the business, and others. A special account is compiled to show how the net profit/ loss is divided up, and it's called a profit and loss appropriation account.

17.6   Interest on Drawings and Loans

Drawings is money taken from the business by the owner. In the case of a sole trader, it's withdrawing part of the invested capital, or its part of the profit made. In the case of a partnership, their capital balances remain fixed and nothing is withdrawn from them. We can't say its part of profits since their share is not yet known. It could be a loss at the year end. So the money taken by any of the partners before their share of profit is known is treated as **borrowed**. And normally when you borrow money you pay interest.

So **interest on drawings** is the money charged by the partnership to individual partners who borrow from the business. It's expressed as a percentage of the amount borrowed. However, since it's the partners who decide what to charge themselves, the rate of interest is not as high as the cost of borrowing from a bank.

This interest is an income to the business. However, since it's not earned through the normal trading activities of the business, it's not recorded on the income statement. It's only recorded on the profit and loss appropriation account. It's added to net profit to get the total available for appropriation and shared among the partners as illustrated in the following section.

Interest on Loans: This is a fee paid by the business for using a partner's money that is not capital. A partner's capital contribution does not exceed the agreed amount stated in the partnership dead. So any other money provided by a partner is treated as a loan and the business pays interest that is similar to the one paid on a bank loan. Interest is a normal **business expense** which is deducted on the profit and loss account, before we get the net profit to be appropriated among the partners.

17.7   The Profit And Loss Appropriation Account

The word **appropriation means dividing up. The appropriation account** is compiled to facilitate and record the dividing up of net profit among partners. The first item is net profit or loss from the profit and loss account. We then add interest on drawings to get the total available for appropriation. Next is the interest on capital, the partner's salaries, and what is left is shared among the partners in their profit sharing ratio. In our example the net profit is $19,000, while the interest on drawings is $200

Calculations: If it's agreed that interest on capital is 10% then we calculate 10% for each of the partner's capital contributed.

For example, if a partner like Mike contributed $24,000 and Judy contributed $12,000, we have the interest for Mike being $2,400 and that for Judy being $1,200 at 10%.

The salary for the partners is agreed and recorded in the partnership deed. It's only copied and entered on to the appropriation account. In our example we assume that Mike is paid $1,500 while Judy is paid $3,000.
We finally have the share of residual net profit. We deduct total interest (**TI**) and total salary (**TS**) from net profit (**NP**) in order to remain with residual net profit (**RNP**).

$$RNP = NP - TI - TS$$

Residual net profit is shared among the partners basing on the **profit sharing ratio** agreed and recorded in the partnership deed. This ratio is only applied on residual net profit after deductions have been made. For example, if the profit sharing ratio is two to Mike and one to Judy,(2:1) and the residual net profit is $11,100. The calculations are;

Add the two figures in the **ratio** to get a total which is **3 parts;**
Divide 11,100 by the 3 parts to get 3,700;
Therefore, each part is to get 3,700
Mike with **two parts** gets;   2 x 3,700 = 7,400
Judy with **one part** gets;   1 x 3,700 = 3,700

Alternatively; 2/3 x 11,100 = 7,400   1/3 x 11,100 = 3,700

The appropriation account is illustrated below;

The Profit & Loss Appropriation Account		
Net Profit		19,000
Interest on Drawings		200
Total for Appropriation		19,200
Interest on Capital		
Mike	2,400	
Judy	+1,200	
Total Interest		3,600
Partner's Salaries		
Mike	1,500	
Judy	+3,000	
Total Salaries		4,500
Share of Residual Net Profit		
Mike	7,400	
Judy	+3,700	
Total Residual Net Profit		+11,100
Total Approriation		19,200

If you prefer the horizontal format then the appropriation account looks as illustrated below;

The Horizontal Appropriation Account					
Interest on Capital			Net Profit		19,000
Mike	2,400		Interest on Drawings		200
Judy	+1,200				
		3,600			
Partner's Salaries					
Mike	1,500				
Judy	+ 3,000				
		4,500			
Share of Residual Net Profit					
Mike	7,400				
Judy	+ 3700				
		+11,100			
Total Appropriation		19,200	Total for Appropriation		19,200

A commission on sales is a payment given to partners basing on how much they sold for the business. It's worked out as a percentage of sales value. It's aimed at encouraging them to sell a lot since the more they sell the higher the commission they get.

A commission is given the same treatment like **salaries** on the appropriation account. It's recorded below the salaries and above the share of residual net profit.

EXERCISE 17B.

You are required to prepare a vertical appropriation account from the following information. Harvey contributed $12,000 while Franklin contributed $20,000 to their capital. They are to get an interest of 15% on their capital. It is Harvey who manages the business and gets a salary of $2,700. They agreed to share the profits equally and the profit made for 2005 was $11,000.

Net Loss

In case the business didn't make a profit but a net loss, **no interest** on capital is given to partners. The only payment to partners is their **salaries** and this actually **increases** the amount of loss. So the total net loss is divided up among the partners in their **profit sharing ratio**. This is illustrated below using the same salaries and profit sharing ratio as above, and a net loss of $2,340.

NET LOSS APPROPRIATION ACCOUNT		
Net Loss		2,340
Salaries		
Mike	1,500	
Judy	+ 3,000	
		+ 4,500
Total Loss to be Appropriated		6,840
Share of Net Loss		
Mike (2 ratios)	4,560	
Judy (1 ratio)	+ 2,280	
Total Loss Appropriated		6,840

17.8   Fixed Capital Accounts

In a sole trading business, capital injections and net profit are added to opening capital, and drawings are deducted before we get the new owner's equity. Injections are not limited by anyone. The capital figure keeps on rising and falling and that's why it's called a **fluctuating capital account.** This is not possible in a partnership because the balances on these accounts are supposed to remain fixed. Each partner has their own capital account. The amount should only change if the partners have jointly accepted an injection of extra capital, or a withdrawal by a partner. So we say that partners have **fixed capital accounts.** The interest on capital for the appropriation account is calculated on these fixed capital balances. Below is an illustration of the fixed capital accounts;

Mike's Capital Account

	Balance b/d	24,000

Judy's Capital Account

	Balance b/d	12,000

The only figures recorded on these accounts is the capital agreed and invested according to the partnership deed. To ensure the amount on each capital account remains fixed, a special account was set up for recording items that would cause the balance to change. The special account is the **current account.**

17.9   Current Accounts

This is an account set up for recording what is due (to be paid) to a partner, and what the partner owes the business. What is due is their interest on capital, salary, and share of residual net profit. What they owe the business are drawings and interest on drawings.

Here are some figures for compiling the vertical current accounts. Mike had a credit balance of $470, while Judy had a debit balance of $120 as opening balances on their current accounts. Mike made drawings for $6,500, while Judy drew $8,000. The other information is extracted from the profit and loss appropriation account in section 17.6 above. Please note that for simplicity, we have excluded interest on drawings. Below is an illustration;

	Mike	Judy
Balance b/d	470	-120
Interest on capital	2,400	1,200
Salaries	1,500	3,000
RNP	+ 7,400	+ 3,700
	11,770	7,780
Drawings	- 6,500	- 8,000
Balance c/d	5,270 Cr	220 Dr
		OR (220)

We start with balances b/d from the previous trading period. If it's a debit balance then it's said to be a **negative balance** and that's when the partner owes the business. If it's a credit balance then it's said to be a **positive balance** and that is when the business owes the partner. Whether it's a positive or negative balance they are recorded on the same line, and only differentiated by either a positive or negative sign. The negative sign is often substituted with brackets. If there is no sign then it's a positive figure.

We add interest on capital, salaries and the share of residual net profit, before deducting drawings.   We are left with a positive or negative balance. A positive balance is differentiated by writing **"Cr"** after the amount, and a negative balance is differentiated by writing **"Dr"** after the amount, or it's put in **brackets**. The balances on the current accounts are then recorded on the balance sheet.

In case of a net loss, the current accounts will only show the salaries, the appropriated loss, drawings, and the final **debit balance**. Debit balances reduce the capital in the business.

Interest on drawings charged to each partner is deducted from their current account before calculating how much is due to each of them.

The Horizontal Format
Using the horizontal format, what is due to a partner is recorded on the credit side while what they owe is debited to the account as illustrated below;

Mike's Current Account

Drawings	6,500	Balance b/d	470
		Interest on capital	2,400
		Salary	1,500
Balance c/d	5,270	SRNP	7,400
	11,770		11,770
		Balance b/d	5,270

Judy's Current Account

Balance b/d	120	Interest on capital	1,200
Drawings	8,000	Salary	3,000
		SRNP	3,700
		Balance c/d	220
	8,120		8,120
Balance b/d	220		

We have a separate account for each partner.
We start by recording the opening balances. If it's a credit balance then its b/d on the credit side. That is what is owed to the partner and its illustrated on Mike's account. If it's a debit balance then its b/d on the debit side. That's what the partner owes and it's illustrated on Judy's account. What is due to a partner's is recorded on the **credit side**. These accounts are balanced and the balance may be on the debit side, credit side, or no balance at all.

If the balance is b/d on the debit side like the one on Judy's account then it's said to be a **debit balance**. This implies the partner owes that balance to the business since they owe or drew more than what is due to them.

If the closing balance is b/d on the credit side like the one on Mike's account then it's said to be a **credit balance**. This implies the business owes that balance to the partner since they owe or drew less than what is due to them.

The Columnar Format
This is very similar to the horizontal format and the principle used is the same. The only difference is that the two or three horizontal accounts are reduced to one account and each of the partners is just given a column on both the debit and credit sides of the account as illustrated below;

	Mike	Judy		Mike	Judy
Balance b/d		120	Balance b/d	470	
Drawings	6,500	8,000	Interest on capital	2,400	1,200
			Salary	1,500	3,000
			SRNP	7,400	3,700
Balance c/d	5,270		Balance c/d		220
	11,770	8,120		11,770	8,120
Balance b/d		220	Balance b/d	5,270	

EXERCISE 17C.

Using the information provided in exercise 17B and the appropriation account you compiled, you are required to prepare vertical current accounts. Harvey had a credit balance of $350 and made drawings of $6,000, while Franklin had a debit balance of $200 and made drawings of $4,000.

17.10   The Balance Sheet

Like a sole trader, a partnership compiles a list of assets, liabilities, and capital at the end of the year. This balance sheet is very similar to the one compiled by a sole trader, and the only differences are with the capital employed section as illustrated below;

THE PARTNERSHIP BALANCE SHEET		
Fixed Assets		
Furniture and fittings		12,500
Motor vehicles		27,000
Equipment		+ 5,800
TFA		45,300
Current Assets		
Stock	3,300	
Debtors	6,480	
Bank	7,900	
Cash	+ 570	
TCA	18,250	
Current Liabilities		
Creditors	- 2,500	
NCA		+ 15,750
Net Assets		61,050
Fixed Capital Balances		
Mike		24,000
Judy		+ 12,000
		36,000
Current Account Balances		
Mike	5,270	
Judy	+ (220)	
Net Current Account Balance		+ 5050
Owner's Equity		41,050
Loan		+ 20,000
Capital Employed		61,050

Instead of having the owner's equity as one figure, we have **separate fixed capital figures** for each partner. In addition to that, we have the **current account balances** and this is shown for each partner. The partner's debit balances on the current account are negative figures and they are recorded in brackets on the balance sheet.

Since the partners have debit (negative) and credit (positive) balances on their current accounts, we get the net balance by deducting the negative from the positive figures. If the negatives are bigger then the net balance is a negative. If the positives are bigger then it's a positive as above. The net balance is added to fixed capital balances before we get the partnership equity. As for the Net Assets section of the balance sheet, it's exactly the same as that of a sole trader.

EXERCISE 17D.
Using the information provided in exercise 17B and 17C including the answers prepared, compile the capital section of the partnership's balance sheet. Please consider that the partnership had a loan of $5,000 from the bank.

Multiple Choice & Short Answer Questions
1. The minimum number of partners in a partnership is
A. 7   B. 2   C. 20   D. 5
2. The maximum number of partners in a partnership is
A. 20   B. 70   C. 50   D. 2
3. If three people start a partnership, the balance sheet will show:
A. One capital account balance   B. Two capital account balances
C. Three capital account balances.   D. None of the above.
4. The partnership appropriation account is where
A. The gross profit of the partnership is calculated.
B. The net profit of the partnership is calculated.
C. The cost of sales of the partnership is calculated.
D. The net profit of the partnership is shared.
5. Which of the following is not written for a sole trader?
A. Appropriation account   B. Trading account
C. Profit and loss account   D. Debtor's ledger
6. Which of the following doesn't appear on the profit and loss appropriation account?
A. Interest on capital   B. Drawings
C. Residual profit   D. Partner's salaries
7. When a partner takes less from a business than what is due to them then their account will have a
A. Credit balance   B. Debit balance
C. Zero balance   D. Negative balance
8. Since we have to maintain fixed capital accounts, the partner's share of profit is
A. Credited to current accounts   B. Debited to current accounts
C. Credited capital accounts   D. Debited to capital accounts
9. Which of the following is found on a partnership profit and loss account?
A. Capital invested   B. Partner's salaries
C. Drawings   D. Employee's salaries
10. Which account do we use to divide the profit among the partners?
A. Capital account   B. Current account
C. Profit and loss   D. Appropriation account

11. When a partner draws more than their entitlement then their current account has a

A. Credit balance   B. Both balances
C. No balance   D. Debit balance

PPQ 2005

6. *Bhekani and Velaphi are in partnership. Their agreement states the following:*

1. Interest is to be allowed on their fixed capital at the rate of 10% per annum

2. Bhekani is to receive a 10% bonus trading profit, after partner's interest on capital has been deducted.

3. Any remaining profits/ losses are to be shared in the proportions; Bhekani on - third and Velaphi two-thirds.

The following information is available for the year ended 31 Dec 2002.

	Bhekani	**Velaphi**
Fixed capital accounts January 2002	10,500	22,200
Current accounts January 2002	510 Cr	528 Dr
Drawings during 2002	10,800	5,400

The Trading Profit for the year ended 31 December 2001 before taking any of the above details and information into account was £19,000.
Required:
(i) The Profit and loss Appropriation Account for the year ended 31 December 2002
(ii) The Current Accounts of the partners for 2002.   *[15]*

PPQ 2004

5. *Suku and Gcino are in a partnership business. Their partnership deed provides for the following:*

1. Interest is to be allowed to their fixed capitals at the rate of 12% p.a.

2. Suku is to receive a salary of 10205 p.a.

3. Suku is to further receive a bonus of 10% of the net profit after partners interest on capital has been deducted.

4. Any remaining profits / losses are to be shared at the ratio 1:2.

   The following information is available for the year ended 31 Dec 2000.

   Fixed capitals 1st January 2000. Suku 15 000 Cr , Gcino 37000 Cr, additional fixed capital brought by Suku 5000. This capital was brought on 1st July 2000.
Current account opening balances; Suku 850 Cr, Gcino 880 Dr
Drawings during the year 2000; Suku 18 000 Gcino 9000
Their net profit earned during the trading period was 31670.

Required: (1)Y prepare a profit and loss appropriation account for the year ended 31 December 2000.
(2) Prepare Partner's Current accounts for the same year.   [15]

PPQ 2003
6. *The following balances were taken from the partnership business of Simiso and Dumisa.*

	DR	CR
Capital Simiso		46,000
Dumisa		54,500
Current Accounts		
Simiso		3,177
Dumisa	4,642	
Motor Vehicle	39,480	
Furniture	8,372	
Stock	70,250	
Debtors	47,274	
Bank Overdraft		14,291
Creditors		44,050
Loan		8000
	170,018	170,018

You are required to prepare a balance sheet as at 31 December 2001.
(15)

PPQ 2002
3. *Lindie and Joe are trading in a partnership dealing in soft drinks. Their partnership deed provides amongst other items the following information:*
- interest is to be allowed on their fixed capitals at the rate of 12% per annum
- Lindie is to receive a bonus of 10% immediately the interest on Capital has been deducted from net profit for the year.
- Any remaining profits/ losses are to be shared in the ratio.
Lindie 1/3   Joe 2/3
The following information is available for the year ended 31 Dec 2000
Fixed Capital accounts:
Lindie   E15000 Cr   Joe   E37000 Cr
Additional Capital brought in by Lindie on 1st July 2000 was E5000
Current accounts in Jan 2000:
Lindie   E850   Joe   E880
Drawings during 2000:
Lindie   E18000   Joe   E9000
The Trading Profit for the year ended 31st December 2000, before taking any of the above additional information into account was E31 670.

Required: *Prepare the profit and loss Appropriation account for the year ending 31 Dec 2000. Show all your workings.*   [15]

PPQ 2001

6. *Fakudze and Radebe are equal partners in a business with capitals of   Fakudze   R7,000   Radebe   R6,000 According to their partnership agreement each partner is entitled to 6% per annum interest on capital before dividing profits. On 31st December 1998 the following balances were extracted from their ledger for the year ended on that date.*

Purchases	55,650	Light and heat	370
Sales	68,960	Sundry expenses	140
Stock (January 1998)	9,600	Carriage outwards	490
Travelling expenses	720	Carriage inwards	180
Rent and rates	2,820	Furniture and fittings	1,600
Insurance	80		

Note the following adjustments.
i) Stock at 31 December 1998 was valued at R8,500.
ii) Rates due on 31 December 1998 but not yet paid R280.
iii) Insurance prepaid 31 December 1998 was R30.
iv) Furniture and fittings to be depreciated by 5% per annum.
v) Amount due to Fakudze and respect of travelling expenses incurred on behalf of business R50.
vi) Radebe had taken goods valued R130 from stock but this has not been recorded.
*You are **required** to prepare:*
a) The trading, profit and loss account of the firm for the year ended 31 December 1998.
b) The profit and loss appropriation account for the year ending 31 December 1998.

ANSWERS		
17B Net Profit		11,000
Interest on Capital		
Harvey	1,800	
Franklin	3,000	
		4,800
Partner' Salaries		
Harvey	2,700	
Share of R N.P		2,700
Harvey	1,750	
Franklin	1,750	
		3,500
N.P Appropriated		11,000

17C

	Harvey	Franklin
Balances b/d	350	(200)
Interest on Capital	1,800	3,000
Salaries	2,700	
SRNP	1,750	1,750
	6,600	4,550
Drawings	6,000	4,000
Closing Balance	600 Cr	550 Cr

17D Capital Section of Balance Sheet

Fixed Capital Accounts		
Harvey		12,000
Franklin		20,000
		32,000
Current Account Balances		
Harvey	600	
Franklin	550	
		1,150
Owner's Equity		33,150
Loan from Bank		5,000
Capital Employed		38,150

NON-PROFIT ORGANISATIONS

18.1   Introduction

Non-profit making organisations [NPO] are set up for the benefit of their members or helping the needy, but **not to make profit**. When members set up a social club, one of the aims is having their own recreation facility. One of the aims of setting up a cooperative society is to find market for their products. A charity may be set up to help the needy by providing them with food, clothing, and other sorts of help. Other examples are associations and religious bodies. However, if any profit is generated from their activities, it's not distributed among the members but re-invested in the organisation to improve/ expand the existing facilities or services. The profit making organisations are businesses which are set up with the major aim of making profit. The profits are shared out among the owners of the business and examples are sole traders and partnerships.

18.2   Sources Of Income

The sole trader and partnership have their source of income being the sales revenue, commissions, rent received, and others. The sources of income for Non-profit making organisations include; membership fees, subscriptions, grants, donations, functions, and trading activities. Although Non-profit making organisations like missionary hospitals charge some money for the services they provide, their aim is not to make profit but to meet the cost of providing the service. Below is an explanation for the different sources of income.

Membership fees: This is money paid by those who want to become members of a club, society or association. It's normally paid once at the time of joining.

Subscriptions: This is a monthly or yearly financial contribution by members to the organisation. Most organisations have both a membership fee and a subscription fee.

Grants: This is a financial contribution from the government or local council, which helps the organisation to meet its financial requirements. It's free money that doesn't have to be paid back.

Donations: This is a financial contribution from individuals and other organisations. It's similar to a grant and it's also free money.

Functions: These are activities organised to raise some money for the organisation and they include dinners, concerts, dances, competitions, raffle draws, and others. They are arranged by organisations which don't get enough income to finance their expenses. The income they get in **excess** of their expenses on the function is a profit. The profit is what constitutes an income and if it's a loss then it's an expense.

Trading Activities: These are the buying and selling activities set up to generate profit. Although they are non-profit making organisations, they try to make a profit if their income is not enough to meet their expenses. So they set up shops, bars, canteens, and others. The profit made is an extra source of income.

18.3   Expenditure

The expenditures incurred by Non-profit making organisations are similar to those for a business. The only difference is that these are **not for profit purposes,** they are aimed at providing or improving their services. They include rent and electricity for their premises, salaries and wages for their staff, stationery for office use, sundry expenses, and others depending on the nature of the organization.

18.4   Record Keeping

Non-profit making organisations keep accounting records for use by their members, beneficiaries, financiers, and others. Many of them are small and managed by a committee of unpaid elected officials. One member is elected as **Treasurer** and given the responsibility of keeping financial records. Since they are not profit making, their records are simplified. The smaller organisations where the Treasurer has little or no Accounting knowledge, they only keep the analysed cashbook that is summarised into a receipts and payments account as their final account. The bigger ones add an income and expenditure statement. The larger ones with better funding employ bookkeepers and accountants, and keep records similar to those of a business.

An analysed cashbook is illustrated below:

AN ANALYSED CASHBOOK

Date	Details	Total	subscriptions	Donations	Membership fee	Dinner Income
1	Bal b/d	1,200				
3	Evelyn	100	50		50	
4	Donor	550		550		
5	Dinner	5,300				5,300
10	Donor	280		280		
13	Anthony	100	50		50	
19	Anne	100	50		50	
20	Dinner	4,700				4,700
21	Donor	640		640		
25	Alex	100	50		50	
		13,070	200	1,470	200	10,000
	Bal b/d	13,070				
		7,365				

Date	Details	Total	Sponsorship	Dinner Expense	Rent	Wages	Electricity	Stationery
2	Pens	85						85
5	Richard	500	500					
6	Dinner	550		550				
12	Rose	500	500					
18	Gerald	500	500					
20	Dinner	450		450				
22	Agnes	500	500					
29	Electricity	320					320	
30	Rent	1,200			1,200			
30	Wages	1,100				1,100		
	Bal c/d	5,705	2,000	1,000	1,200	1,100	320	85
		7,365						
		13,070						

Each of the regular receipts and expenditures is allocated a column. So each amount is recorded twice, once in the total column and once in the allocated column. The recording in the allocated column is to ease the getting of the column total for preparing the receipts and payments account. The recording in the totals column is to facilitate the balancing of the cashbook.

18.5   The Receipts And Payments Account

The receipts and payments account is a **classified summary** of the transactions recorded in the cashbook. It starts with the cashbook balance brought down, and ends with the closing balance for the period. It shows the totals of the classified **in flows** (receipts) and **out flows** (payments) of cash from the organisation.

Below is a receipts and payments account, it's a summary of the analysed cashbook above.

California Club's Receipts and Payments Account

1	Balance b/d	1,200	School fees	2,000
	Subscriptions	200	Dinner expenses	1,000
	Donations	1,470	Rent	1,200
	Membership fees	200	wages	1,100
	Dinner income	10,000	Electricity	320
			Stationary	85
			Balance c/d	7,365
		13,070		13,070
	Balance b/d	7,365		

All the **receipt totals** are recorded on the debit side, while the **payment totals** are recorded on the credit side. If the details are recorded in an ordinary cashbook then the receipts have to be grouped and added under the different group headings. For example, all membership fees are added together and we only have their total on the receipts and payments account. All subscriptions, all donations, and other types of income are added in their respective categories. The same applies to the credit side where we have payments grouped and added in their respective categories. This account is balanced and the balances must be the same as the ones in the cashbook since it's just a summary.

EX 18A   Hospice at Home's Cashbook

1	Balance b/d	397	1	Medicine	96
2	Membership	32	2	Food	138
3	Donation	470	3	Motor expenses	90
7	Membership	32	8	Medicine	120
9	Donation	330	9	Food	140
16	Membership	32	10	Motor expenses	88
17	Donation	290	15	Medicine	140
20	Donation	550	16	Food	260
21	Membership	32	17	Motor expenses	75
26	Donation	240	22	Medicine	80
			23	Food	190
			24	Motor expenses	57
			31	Balance c/d	931
		2,405			2,405
31	Balance b/d	931			

Write a receipts and payments account from this cashbook.

18.6   Income And Expenditure Statement

An income and expenditure statement is prepared to show results of the financial activities which took place during the year. It shows the effect of these activities on the total finances of the organisation. While the profit-making organisations prepare a trading, profit and loss account, the non-profit making organisations prepare an income and expenditure statement as one of their final accounts. The two are prepared following the same principle of deducting expenses from incomes, to determine if there is a profit /loss for the business, or a surplus /deficit for the non-profit making organisation.

The income and expenditure statement is prepared using information from the receipts and payments account, plus any explanatory notes or adjustments. However, we only use **revenue incomes and revenue expenditures**. Not all receipts are incomes, and not all payments are expenditures. For example, receipts from the sale of assets are not an income. The purchase of assets is not an expenditure, what is recorded for fixed assets is depreciation. Please note that this statement requires **income earned** and not income received, and **expenses incurred** and not expenses paid. Therefore, some adjustments similar to those for a business are made. Below is an illustration of an income and expenditure statement;

California Club's Income and Expenditure Statement for the year ended 31 December 2004		
Incomes		
Dinner sales		10,000
Donations		1,470
Subscriptions		200
Membership Fees		200
Total Incomes		11,870
Expenditure		
Rent Paid	1,200	
School Fees	2,000	
Wages	1,100	
Dinner Expenses	1,000	
Stationery	85	
Electricity	320	
Total Expenditure		5,705
Surplus of Income over Expenditure		6,165

Expenditures are deducted from incomes and if the answer is **positive** then it's said to be an **excess of income over expenditure**. It means the organisation received more income than its expenditure and we refer to it as **a surplus**. A business refers to this as **net profit**. If the answer is **negative** then it's said to be an **excess of expenditure over income** and it's a **deficit**. It means the organisation received less income compared to its expenditure. A business refers to this as **net loss**.

It's only the incomes and expenditures for the year that should be recorded on the income and expenditure statement. The income and expenditures for the previous year and those for the following year are excluded and this is part of the adjustments made.

Differences between the	
Receipts and Payments Account and &	**Income and Expenditure Statement**
1. it shows the actual cash received and paid out	1. it shows incomes earned and expenses incurred after adjustments to actual receipts and expenses
2. It mixes up the capital and revenue items	2. It only deals with revenue incomes and revenue expenditure
3. It only shows a cash balance or overdrawn balance	3. It shows whether there was a surplus or deficit

EX 18B.
Using the following figures, compile an income and expenditure statement. Rent paid 750   subscriptions   1,760
school fees 3,200   donations received 2,780   wages   800

stationery   94   *membership fees*   370   *electricity*   188
medicines 460   *raffle draw profits* 4,369

18.7   The Trading Account

The profits made from functions and trading activities are treated as an income, while a loss is treated as an expense on the income and expenditure statement. However, to determine if a profit or loss was made from a particular activity, we compile a separate trading account for **each** profit generating activity like dinners, the bar, restaurant, canteen, sale of refreshments, and others.

When compiling the trading account we need the cost of stock or service sold, and the proceeds from sales to get the gross profit or loss. If there are any direct expenses on the activity then we deduct them from gross profit to get net profit. It's the gross or net profit that is added to the other incomes on the income and expenditure statement. If it's a loss then it's deducted. This means the detail of incomes and expenses on income generating activities are not recorded on the income and expenditure statement, it's only the profit or loss from a particular activity.

This trading account is compiled basing on the same principle as the one for a business. Below is an illustration of a trading account for a refreshments trading activity;

Califonia Club's Refreshments Trading Account		
Sales of Refreshments		13,815
Opening Stock	470	
Purchases (derived below)	4,850	
Goods available for sale	5,320	
Closing Stock	225	
Cost of Goods Sold		5,095
Gross Profit		8,720
Wages(direct expense)		4,800
Profit on Refreshments to Y & E stat.		3,920

18.8   The Accumulated Fund

Instead of capital, the money contributed by members or well wishers to a non-profit organisation is referred to as **accumulated fund**. This fund is an accumulation of subscriptions, membership fees, donations, surpluses, and others, and that is the source of its name. The treatment for accumulated fund is the same as capital in a business, and they are both recorded in the same position on the balance sheet. We use the same formula for capital to derive accumulated fund and it's;

Accumulated Fund = Assets – Liabilities   AF = A – L

The formula for **Capital** = **Assets − Liabilities (C = A − L)**

18.9   The Balance Sheet

This is a statement compiled by Non-profit making organisations to show their financial position at a particular date. It's similar to the one compiled by businesses and it shows the accumulated fund (capital), assets, and the liabilities of the organisation. It's one of the final accounts they prepare and below is an illustration.

CALIFORNIA CLUB'S BALANCE SHEET AS AT 31st DEC 2004			
Fixed Assets	**Cost**	**Acc. Depn**	**NBV**
Motor vehicles	30,000	12,000	18,000
Equipment	12,000	4,800	7,200
Total Fixed Assets	42,000	16,800	25,200
Current Assets			
Refreshment stock		225	
Bank		6,788	
Cash		237	
Total Current Assets		7,250	
Current Liabilities			
Expenses due		670	
Net Current Assets			6,580
Net Assets			31,780
Accumulated fund			
Balance at 1 January 2004			16,580
Surplus of income over expenditure			5,200
			21,780
Long Term Liabilities			
Bank Loan			10,000
Funds Employed			31,780

Multiple Choice & Short Answer Questions

1. A club's receipts and payments account is a summary of the?
A. Profit and loss account   B. Appropriation account
C. Cashbook   D. Balance sheet
2. A club's income and expenditure statement is similar to
A. Profit and loss account   B. Appropriation account
C. Cashbook   D. Balance sheet
3. A club's accumulated fund has the same formula as
A. Net profit   B. Gross profit   C. Capital   D. Receipts
4. A receipts and payments account shows the
A. Income earned & expenditure incurred   B. Cash received & paid out
C. Profit or loss   D. Accumulated fund
5. The balance on the receipts and payments account is the balance on the
A. Cashbook   B. Profit and loss account
C. Expenses account   D. Subscriptions account

6. A club's profit is referred to as
A. Net profit   B. Deficit
C. Accumulated fund   D. Surplus
7. A loss made by an association is referred to as
A. Net profit   B. Deficit
C. Accumulated fund   D. Surplus
8. The formula for accumulated fund is
A. Assets + Liabilities   B. Assets – Liabilities
C. Liabilities – Assets   D. Capital – Assets
9. If you get a negative when deducting expenses from incomes then it's a
A. Deficit   B. Surplus   C. Profit   D. Gain

EXERCISE 18C
On 1 January 2000 the S.O.S village had the following assets:
Cash at bank $500   *Buildings $22,300*
During the year to 31 December 2000 the village received and paid
the following amounts:

RECEIPTS		PAYMENTS	
Balance b/d	500	Rent and rates	2,400
Subscriptions	4,700	Accounting fees	300
Vistors fees	3,400	Interest on loan	600
Lottery income	1,500	Pool tables	2,500
		Balance c/d	4,300
	10,100		10,100
Balance b/d	4,300		

The pool tables are to be depreciated by 15%.
Required: *(a) Prepare the village's income and expenditure*
account for the year to 31 December 2000.
(a)Prepare the Balance Sheet as at 31 December 2000.

EXERCISE 18D.
The Salmon Hunters Club owned assets as follows on 1ˢᵗ Jan 2003.
Cash at bank   2,000   Canteen stock   1,000
Club House   15,200
Below is their receipts and payments account.

RECEIPTS		PAYMENTS	
Balance b/d	2,000	Equipment	5,000
Canteen income	6,200	Rent	2,000
Miscellaneous fees	3,100	Canteen stock	4,120
Subscriptions	8,880	Canteen expenses	750
		Stationery	400
		Telephones	820
		Balance c/d	7,090
	20,180		20,180
Balance b/d	7,090		

Further information was available as follows:
1.   Canteen stock at 31ˢᵗ Dec 2003 was worth 926.

2.   380 was due on telephone services.
3.   The equipment is to be depreciated by 1,250.
4.   Rent of 400 is yet to be paid.

Required: Prepare the club's Income and Expenditure account for the year to 31 December 2003 and a balance sheet at the same date.

PPQ 2005
4. (a) From the following information given below, compile a Receipts and Payments Account of the Sibebe Tiger's Club for the year ended 31 December 2000.   (13)

Cash on hand (31 December 1999)	58
Bank (31 December 1999)	277
Subscription received during the year	1484
Wages paid in cash	788
Sundry	69
Donations	636
Rent	320
Cost of balls	72
Stationery	50

(b) (i) What is the difference between a business and non profit organization?   (1)
(ii) How do non profit organizations raise their capital?   (1)

PPQ 2003
5. (a) Define the following:

(i) Surplus   (ii) Deficit   [2]
(b) The following balances were taken from Faka-Sandla Charity Organization. Compile an Income and Expenditure Statement for the year ended 30 June 2001.

Rent paid	750		
Donations	2780		
Stationery	94		
Subscription	1760		
Electricity	188		
School fees	3200		
Membership fee	370		
Medicines	460		
Raffle draw profit	4369		
Wages	800		(15)

PPQ 2002

2. *The Receipts and Payments Account of Bhekinkosi Primary Ladies Club for the year ended 31 December 1990 was as follows:*

Recipts		Payment	
Balance Jan 1990	334	Rent and rates	943
Subscriptions	1420	Postage and stationery	265
Donations	75	Cost of Refreshments	495
Gift (for purchase	230	Sundry Expenses	293
of equipment)		New equipment	403
Sales of Refreshments	713	Wages paid (for	115
		refreshment preperation	
		Balance c/d	258
	2,772		2,772

The following additional information is available

Refreshments Account	
Owing to Suppliers at the beginning of the year	28
Paid during the year	495
Purchases for the year	467

	Jan-90	Dec 31 1990
Stocks of refreshment	39	33
Owing to suppliers for refreshments	28	-
Subscriptions in arrears	-	29
Subscriptions in advance	-	44
Equipment at valuation	374	678
Depreciation of Equipment		
Book value at 1 Jan 1990	374	
New equipment	403	
	777	
Less book value at 31 Dec 1990	678	
Depreciation	99	

You are required:
- to prepare a trading account
- income and expenditure account for the year ended Dec. 31 1990. [15]

PPQ 2001

9. *Prepare an Income and Expenditure account and a Balance Sheet from the details below;*

CASH BOOK OF THE COMMERCE SOCIETY

Cash in hand, 1 Sept.	45	Stationery	12
Subscription for Sept.	416	Coach hire	87
Subscription in advance at 30 Sept.	10	Dance expenses	58
Donations	30	Sweepstake prizes	44
Dance receipts	42	Bookcase	80
Sweepstake sale	96	Sports equipment	246
		Balance, 30 Sept.	112
	639		639

There was an outstanding bill of R15 for coach hire at 30 September. It was decided by the committee to revalue sports equipment at R200. (15)

PPQ 2000

3. *The Treasurer of the Sitamiseni Youth Club prepared the statement on the following page;*
NOTES:
The club has R100 in the bank. Amount owing for electricity is R5. Tents, camping gear owned by the club R100 (the club owned tents worth R40 at 1ˢᵗ January).
a) Is the heading correct?
b) Is the R100 a profit?
c) Draw up in good form Sitanani Youth Club account and a properly headed balance sheet.

BALANCE SHEET FOR THE YEAR ENDING 31st DECEMBER 1999

INCOME		EXPENDITURE	
Cash in hand	30	Raffle Prizes	40
Gate takings	80	Rent of Hall	20
Raffle tickets	100	New Tents	60
Subscriptions	25	Printing of Raffle Tickets	20
Jumble sale	30	Camp Expenditure	125
Annual camp receipts	120	Group Hut rent	20
		Balance profit	100
	385		385

ANSWERS

18A   Hospice at Home's Receipts and Payments Account

1	Balance b/d	397	Medicine	436
	Membership fees	128	Food	728
	Donations	1,880	Motor Expenses	310
			Balance c/d	931
		2,405		2,405
	Balance b/d	931		

18B   Income and Expenditure Statement

Incomes

Subscriptions		1,760
Donations		2,780
Membership Fees		370
Profit from Raffle draws		4,369
Total Incomes		9,279

Expenditures

Rent Paid	750	
School Fees	3,200	
Wages	800	
Stationery	94	
Electricity	188	
Medicines	460	
Total Expenditure		5,492
Surplus of Income over Expenditure		3,787

CHAPTER 19

ACCOUNTING PRINCIPLES AND CONCEPTS

19.1 INTRODUCTION

Accounting Principles and Concepts are rules which lay down the procedure for preparing accounts. They have come to be generally accepted by authorities in the accounting profession, over a long period of time. They were put in place because accounts have to be prepared in a way that is understandable and acceptable to all the different users of accounting information. The interests of the owners, the lenders, the government, the managers, and others, are all catered for, if they are prepared following the same principles and concepts.

The list of Accounting Principles and Concepts is long. However, for this syllabus, we look at the duality concept, money measurement concept, business entity concept, and prudence concept.

19.2 THE DUALITY CONCEPT

The word dual means two. According to this concept, each and every transaction must have **two entries** in the ledger, which are equal and opposite to each other. For every debit entry there is a credit entry. This concept is the basis of the **double entry principle** which we use when recording transactions in the ledger. Every transaction is recorded twice in the ledger, once on the debit side and once on the credit side.

19.5 THE MONEY MEASUREMENT CONCEPT

According to this concept, we only record those aspects of a business that can be expressed in **money terms**. If something can't be expressed in money terms then we can't record it in accounts. For example, if a business has two cows each weighing 500 kilograms, they should be recorded by their money value and not by weight or anything else.

According to this concept, barter trade and any other transactions which don't use money as the medium of exchange cannot be recorded. Barter Trade is the exchange of goods for other goods or services without the use of money. For example, you may get a cow by giving away 5 goats.

19.4   THE BUSINESS ENTITY CONCEPT

According to this concept, the business and its owner are treated as **separate entities**. The personal activities of the owner do not concern the business and are not recorded in the accounts of the business. The business should pay its own expenses and debts, and the owner should pay their own expenses and debts.

This is the reason why capital contributed by the owner is also a **liability**. It belongs to the owner and not the business. What the business owns are the assets. The owner is not the business, although they may act on behalf of the business. The only time when personal issues are recorded in the accounts is when they contribute capital, or when they take drawings. Any personal expenses paid by the business are recorded as drawings and they are not taken to the profit and loss account.

19.5   THE PRUDENCE CONCEPT

According to this concept, **profits should never be anticipated until they are realised**. However, **foreseeable losses should be accounted for immediately**. In the absence of actual figures, a best estimate is made and this is the principle in use when provisions are made.   The financial statements should be fairly accurate.   The gains or incomes should not be overstated by ignoring foreseeable losses or expenses. Revenue or income should not be recorded before it's earned. This concept emphasizes caution when dealing with uncertainty.

The provision for bad debts is based on this concept. There is no point in overstating profits when there is good reason to believe that some debtors will not pay. Apart from bad debts written off, there are some outstanding debtors who will not pay. When they don't pay it becomes a loss and an expense that reduces profit. Therefore, since this loss is foreseen and expected, it should be accounted for immediately.

However, since we don't know the exact amount, a best estimate is made in form of a provision. This provision is transferred from the profit and loss account, to the provision for doubtful debts account to be utilized the following year, when the bad debts are written off.

Multiple Choice & Short Answer Questions

1. Which accounting concept assumes the business will continue operating in the foreseeable future ?

A. Duality   B. Going Concern
C. Prudence   D. Conservation

2. Which concept says that we should stick to one particular way of recording?
A. Consistency   B. Duality
C. Conservation   D. Prudence

3. Which accounting concept emphasises the value of what is recorded?
A. Consistency   B. Materiality
C. Accruals   D. Matching

4. Which accounting concept talks about double entry?
A. Matching   B. Accruals
C. Consistency   D. Duality

5. The historical cost concept says that assets should be recorded at the
A. Replacement cost   B. Inflated cost
C. Original cost   D. Current cost

6. The accounting concept which says that expenses should be compared with revenues for the same period is the ....
A. Matching concept   B. Business entity concept
C. Consistency concept   D. Money measurement concept

7. The concept which says that " foreseeable losses should be accounted for immediately " is?
A. Duality   B. Prudence
C. Accruals   D. Matching

8. Which of the following is not an accounting concept?
A. Duality   B. Prudence
C. Materiality   D. Depreciation

9. Which of the following is an accounting concept?
A. Appropriation   B. Appreciation
C. Contingency   D. Prudence

10. The accounting concept which says that profit is the difference between income earned and expenses incurred and not cash receipts and payments is
A. Matching concept   B. Materiality concept
C. Accruals concept   D. Prudence concept

11. The principle which says that a limited liability company has a separate legal status from its owners is
A. Business entity   B. Accruals
C. Money measurement   D. Prudence

12. Valuing stock at the lower of cost or net realisable value is under the
A. Prudence concept   B. Materiality concept
C. Matching concept   D. Accruals concept

13. Capital contributed by the owner is a liability under which principle?
A. Prudence   B. Accruals
C. Materiality   D. Business entity

14. Which principle requires the creation of a provision for bad debts?
A. Business entity   B. Accruals   C. Prudence   D. Materiality

15. Which concept says that even if an asset doesn't legally belong to the business it should be recorded on the balance sheet?
A. Prudence   B. Accruals
C. Materiality   D. Substance over form

19. Which of the following is guided by both the prudence concept and the matching concept?

A. Expense due   B. Advance income

C. Overcast   D. Bad debts provision

17. Which of the following is not based on the prudence concept?

A. Discounts provision   B. Expense provision

C. Depreciation provision   D. Bad debts provision

18. According to the realisation concept, which of the following is recognized on sending an invoice?

A. Income   B. Expenses

C. Payment date   D. Bad debt

19. According to the time interval concept, financial statements should be prepared   every?

A. 6 months   B. Month   C. 12 months   D. Decade

20. According to the matching concept, which of the following is not deducted from sales?

A. Opening stock   B. Closing stock

C. Purchases   D. Cost of sales

21. What is meant by accounting concepts? Provide an explanation for five accounting concepts that you know.

22. State why stock is normally valued at the lower of cost or net realisable value when final accounts are prepared.

Printed in the United States
134356LV00005B/32/A